Sinatra
101

Sinatra
101

THE 101 BEST RECORDINGS
AND THE STORIES BEHIND THEM

ED O'BRIEN
WITH
ROBERT WILSON

FOREWORD BY SID MARK

BOULEVARD BOOKS
New York

Photos on pages 1, 9, 37, and 113 courtesy of Charles Pignone Collection.
Photo on page 168 courtesy of "Mitzi."
Lyrics to "Hey Look, No Crying" reprinted with kind permission of Susan Birkenhead.

SINATRA 101: THE 101 BEST RECORDINGS AND
THE STORIES BEHIND THEM

A Boulevard Book / published by arrangement with
the authors

PRINTING HISTORY
Boulevard trade paperback edition / September 1996

The Putnam Berkley World Wide Web site address is
http://www.berkley.com

ISBN: 1-57297-165-7

BOULEVARD
Boulevard Books are published by The Berkley Publishing Group,
200 Madison Avenue, New York, New York 10016.
BOULEVARD and its logo are trademarks
belonging to Berkley Publishing Corporation.

PRINTED IN THE UNITED STATES OF AMERICA

10 9 8 7 6 5 4 3 2 1

CONTENTS

CONTENTS

The Capitol Years

CONTENTS

CONTENTS

The Reprise Years

CONTENTS

FOREWORD

Frank Sinatra is an original. Not unlike a Picasso or van Gogh, when Sinatra paints a portrait, the tones and colors are his alone. "It comes to this," wrote Rod McKuen, "whatever kind of man he is, whoever made us, made just one of him."

I do not have the luxury of space in this writing to fully share my innermost feelings for this man I've known for thirty-seven years. Is it not true, whether on record or on stage, that he sings to all of us individually, that he sings to you and me, to all of us who have wanted it all? He takes words on a music sheet and brings them to life. I've heard him smile on "The Best Is Yet to Come" and cry on "I'm a Fool to Want You." His songs to me are like a mirror reflecting moments in all our lives.

Everyone knows that Frank Sinatra is the consummate performer. To me, he is also the consummate friend. There are no boundaries to his loyalty. Whether it be an introduction from the stage, a phone call after a hospital stay, or a congratulatory note after a TV profile, Frank is there. We've broken bread together. We've lifted a glass or two. The only thing I ever asked for—his friendship—he's given me. It's a gift I will always treasure.

SID MARK

ACKNOWLEDGMENTS

The authors wish to thank the following researchers, players, and collectors whose help and expertise were instrumental in the preparation of *Sinatra 101*.

The Researchers

Nat Shapiro and Bruce Pollack, editors of *Popular Music 1920–1979*, published by Gale Research Inc., Detroit; Joel Whitman, author of *Pop Memories 1890–1954*, published by Record Research Inc., Menomonee Falls, Wisconsin; Roy Hemming, author of *The Melody Lingers On: The Great Song Writers and Their Movie Musicals*, published by Newmarket Press, New York; Robert Kimball, editor of *The Complete Lyrics of Cole Porter*, published by Alfred A. Knopf, Inc., New York; Max Wilk, author of *They're Playing Our Song*, published by Atheneum, New York; Miles Kreuger, Institute of the American Musical, Los Angeles; the RCA, Columbia, Capitol, and Reprise archives and personnel, including Christine Flores, JoAnn Devito, Lee Herschberg, Jo Motta, Joe McEwen, Bernadette Moore, Nathaniel Brewster, Hank Cattaneo, and others; the Albany Public Library, Albany, New York; Gene Lees, editor and publisher of *Jazzletter*, Ojai, California; and Harry Locke.

The Players

Nelson Riddle; Billy May; Don Costa; Gordon Jenkins; Neal Hefti; Bill Miller; Al Viola; Tony Mottola; Vincent Falcone, Jr.; Susan Birkenhead; Frank Sinatra, Jr.; Jule Styne; and Joe Malin.

The Collectors

Richard Apt; Henry Bottieri; James Cochran; Wayne Connors; Gregory Dispenza; Ric Forrest; George Fraser; Joan Gillen; David Hirschler; Charlie Jones; Sid Mark; Giuseppe Marcucci; Maryann Mastrodonato; Richard Rubino; Alex Sazak; Walter Scott; Michael Schnurr; Jonathan Schwartz; Robert Sherrick; Edmund G. Teixeira; and Anthony Renaud.

INTRODUCTION

Sinatra 101 is a guide to the 101 all-time best recordings of Frank Sinatra. This should not be confused with the singer's greatest hits.

To choose just 101 recordings out of Sinatra's sprawling body of work was a problem from the onset. To date, Sinatra has recorded 1,414 songs in a career that spans seven decades. This does not include promotional work and concert recordings.

In the final mix, we decided to include three recordings from Sinatra's RCA years, seventeen from the Columbia years, fifty-two from the Capitol years, and twenty-nine from the Reprise years. The songs are arranged chronologically in the text, from number 1 to 101, beginning with the May 23, 1940, recording of "I'll Never Smile Again" and ending with "It's Sunday," recorded on February 28, 1983. This arrangement creates a residual feature—a time line. This enables the reader to "see" the evolution of the singer and his artistry.

Sinatra's best work is timeless. We believe *Sinatra 101* captures the essence of his artistry, and its lasting contribution to a great American art form. The criteria applied in selecting these particular recordings were as follows: 1) outstanding vocal performance; 2) songs and/or themes especially significant in the context of American popular music and the culture it embodies; and 3) the enduring quality of the overall work. An exceptional vocal performance did not automatically qualify a song for inclusion. A substandard tune is still just that, no matter how well it is sung. We agonized over many of our selections and we had long discussions with other Sinatra authorities regarding the merit of our choices. The rigid criteria we employed are designed to ensure a group of definitive recordings for any collector of classical American pop.

Each recording, or entry, includes the following basic components: song title; name(s) of lyricist and composer; date and location of the recording; name of arranger; and title of compact disc (CD) on which the recording appears, including CD catalog number. Also included are titles and catalog numbers of CDs that include other versions of the same song by Sinatra. Each entry also contains information that draws from several or all of the following: details and/ or anecdotes from the recording session itself; the history of the song; Sinatra's reading and interpretation of the song; the development and effect of the arrangement; the importance of the song in the framework of Sinatra's career and life; and notable events recounted by those who were part of, or present at, the recording session.

Lest the songs in *Sinatra 101* be the sole opinion of the authors, we asked a panel of Sinatra experts to identify for us their all-time favorite Sinatra recordings. These experts are Billy May, the great arranger who charted many of Sinatra's finest recordings; Bill Miller, Sinatra's piano player and confidant for over forty years; Al Viola, Sinatra's guitarist for more than twenty years; Tony Mottola, who served Sinatra as both guitarist and arranger and who knew the singer in the nickel-and-dime days when they worked for carfare money; Sid Mark, the host since 1955 of *The Sounds of Sinatra,* the nationally syndicated radio program heard on more than one hundred stations coast to coast; Jonathan Schwartz, the brilliant musicologist whose *Sinatra Saturday* radio program is broadcast each week by station WQEW in New York; Tony Renaud, radio personality and intimate friend of the Sinatra family; and others. Their personal selections are included in the book.

So what is this thing about Sinatra? What is it that separates him from all other singers in the history of American popular music? The answer is quite simple. Just listen.

Sinatra 101 is a beginning. Enjoy.

ED O'BRIEN
ROBERT WILSON

THE
RCA
YEARS

1

``I'll Never Smile Again''

Words and music by Ruth Lowe
Recorded May 23, 1940, in New York City
Arranged by Fred Stulce
CD: *The Song Is You* (RCA 07863-66353-2)

Sinatra's first major hit. With its prophetic lyrics, "I'll Never Smile Again" would crystallize the yearning and despair of a generation torn apart by World War II. Recorded with Tommy Dorsey and His Orchestra, to an arrangement by saxophone player Fred Stulce, the track features a near-perfect tempo, a sweet solo by Dorsey, and marvelous harmonies between Sinatra and the Pied Pipers. The song was number one on the *Billboard* chart for twelve consecutive weeks.

For the next forty years, Sinatra performed the song on radio, television, and in concert. It was among the eleven songs he personally selected and performed at his "retirement concert" on June 13, 1971. Sinatra would do two more studio recordings of the song: on May 14, 1959, for Capitol, available on *No One Cares* (CDP 7-94519-2) and *The Capitol Years* (C2-94777); and for Reprise on October 11, 1965, available on *A Man and His Music* (Rep. CD 1016-2).

*T*here is a recording of "I'll Never Smile Again" from April 23, 1940, but there is considerable debate on whether it has ever been commercially issued. The RCA work sheets indicate that it has been. A New York newspaper article from the spring of 1940 by columnist Earl Wilson announces the release. Still, many Sinatra scholars claim the recording has never been issued.

2

"Without a Song"

Words by Edward Eliscu and Billy Rose, music by Vincent
  Youmans
Recorded January 20, 1941, in New York City
Arranged by Sy Oliver
CD: *The Song Is You* (RCA 07863-66353-2)

The apprentice was learning from the master. Sinatra had been with the Tommy Dorsey band for more than a year, a disciple of the band leader and his seamless trombone playing. The phenomenal breath control exhibited by Sinatra throughout his career is never more apparent than it is on "Without a Song." As Dorsey historian Walter Scott observed, "The extended linking of phrases throughout the song displays in abundance what Sinatra had learned from TD." The great Sinatra recordings waiting to be done would possess an effortless style—a technique honed with Dorsey.

At four minutes and twenty-five seconds, "Without a Song" is Sinatra's longest solo track with Dorsey. The song is a paean to the glory of the written word set to music. The sweetness of Sinatra's voice enhances the melodic line and his tender and careful phrasing heightens the impact of the lyrics.

Sinatra performed the song many times throughout his career. He recorded the tune again on May 2, 1961, available on *I Remember Tommy* (Rep. CD 9-45267-2) and *The Reprise Collection* (Rep. CD 9-26340-2). A live recording at the Olympia in Paris on June 5, 1962, is available on *Sinatra and Sextet: Live in Paris* (Rep. CD 9-45487-2). Two more recordings were made but never released: for Reprise on March 20, 1961, and in concert at the Sands Hotel in Las Vegas on November 5, 1961.

---

*S*inatra caught the ear of band leader Harry James in June 1939. The occasion was a radio remote broadcast from the Rustic Cabin, a roadhouse located on the outskirts of Alpine, New Jersey, not far from the Palisades, where the twenty-three-year-old Sinatra had been working for two years as a waiter, emcee, and singer. James, the former trumpet player for Benny Goodman, had just started his own band and was looking for a vocalist. Sinatra accepted the offer. A month later, in July 1939, Sinatra was in the studio, recording "From the Bottom of My Heart" and "Melancholy Mood" for the Brunswick label.

3

"In the Blue of Evening"

Words by Tom Adair and music by Alfred D'Artega
Recorded June 17, 1942, in New York City
Arranged by Axel Stordahl
CD: *The Song Is You* (RCA 07863-66353.2)

Sinatra's finest recording with Tommy Dorsey. Recorded near the end of his tenure with the band, the performance is a culmination of all that Sinatra had been training for. The "band singer" was now an artist in his own right. He had been voted the most popular male vocalist in *Downbeat*'s readers' poll—and he was ready to graduate.

In this recording, Sinatra displays his technical mastery of the art of popular singing. The phrasing, breath control, intonation, timbre, and vocal range of Sinatra on this track would become the foundation of his musical artistry.

A magnificent live recording, an air check taken from a radio broadcast of August 6, 1942, is also available on *The Song Is You*. Sinatra recorded "In the Blue of Evening" again on March 21, 1961, released in 1992 on *I Remember Tommy* (Rep. CD 9-45267-2). An unissued version of the song was recorded for Reprise on May 2, 1961, but there is no complete master from the session.

*I*n an article he wrote for *Metronome* magazine, published in October 1943, Sinatra revealed the names of his favorite vocalists. Six of the ten singers receiving the highest accolades from Sinatra were women.

Interestingly, the qualities Sinatra cited in several female singers would later become foundations of his own artistry. Of Mildred Bailey: "She makes with vocal tricks, but also feels the song and uses her knowledge of arrangements in her interpretations." Of Ella Fitzgerald: "for her whimsical style and originality." And of Dinah Shore: "She is a fine vocalist who puts a tremendous amount of feeling, understanding and expression into every note she sings."

At the top of Sinatra's list was Bing Crosby. "The Great Man brought to music what has grown into an American institution," Sinatra wrote. "I know that I am indebted to him for the inspiration he has given me and I must admit that I'm probably one of his first and most enthusiastic rooters."

THE
COLUMBIA
YEARS

4

"All the Things You Are"

Words by Oscar Hammerstein II and music by Jerome Kern
Recorded July 8, 1944, in Hollywood
Arranged by Axel Stordahl
CD: *Frank Sinatra—The V-Discs* (C2K-66135-CK-66136)

A track recorded by Sinatra at a special V-disc session in the summer of 1944 during a musicians strike. Prevented from recording in the studio with a live band, the singer gave freely of his time for the U.S. government's victory disc program, which provided GIs overseas with recordings from back home. The vocal reading by Sinatra on this recording is particularly outstanding. It ends on an uncharacteristically high note for Sinatra—but he nails it.

When they composed "All the Things You Are," Hammerstein and Kern were at the apex of their songwriting brilliance. "The dearest things I know are what you are" is one of the greatest romantic lines ever written. The play for which it was composed, *Very Warm for May*, was as much a failure as this exquisite song was a success.

The song was part of the Sinatra lexicon throughout the 1940s. He recorded it for Columbia on January 29, 1945. Despite a marvelous vocal, the unnecessary choral background undermines the work as a whole. The track is available on *Frank Sinatra—The Columbia Years 1943–1952* (CXK-48673-CK-52867) and on *The Voice—The Columbia Years* (C4K-40343-CK-40632). In the late 1980s, Sinatra

11

included the song in concert rehearsals, but he did not perform it on stage.

$\mathcal{S}$inatra the teenage idol was the catalyst for the Columbus Day riot in New York in 1944. Hoping to see Sinatra perform at the five-thousand-seat Paramount Theater, about thirty thousand fans jammed the streets in and around Times Square. When the news reached the crowd that the show was sold out, things got ugly. Frustration and anger degenerated into vandalism, and additional police were called in to help restore order.

5

"Embraceable You"

Words by Ira Gershwin and music by George Gershwin
Recorded December 19, 1944, in Hollywood
Arranged by Axel Stordahl
CD: *Frank Sinatra—The Columbia Years 1943–1952* (CXK-
    48673-CK-52867) and *The Voice—The Columbia Years*
    (C4K-40343-CK-40631)

Recordings like "Embraceable You" earned Sinatra the sobriquet "the Voice." Composed by the Gershwins for the 1930 Broadway musical *Girl Crazy*, starring Ethel Merman, the song became a great American standard. But few singers—if any—have been able to bring to the song the ethereal quality that Sinatra delivers here.

The song was part of Sinatra's repertoire for the next half century. There was a second recording on March 3, 1960, a more knowing and sexier version, more suitable for the cynically romantic. It is available on *Nice 'n' Easy* (CDP 7-96827-2) and on *Frank Sinatra—The Capitol Years* (C2-94777 CDP-7-94320-2). Another recording was released in 1994 for *Frank Sinatra Duets II* (CDP 7243-8-28103-2). The orchestral tracks were laid down on May 17 and 18 at the Clinton Studio in New York. The vocal is a composite of live recordings taped during the summer.

One of the more interesting versions of "Embraceable You" was recorded by Sinatra in a promotional film for the American Tobacco Company on July 27, 1947. The singer, backed by The Lucky Strike Quartette, performed the song with the Hit Parade Orchestra.

6

``She's Funny That Way''

Words by Richard Whiting and music by Neil Moret
Recorded December 19, 1944, in Hollywood
Arranged by Axel Stordahl
CD: *Frank Sinatra—The Columbia Years 1943–1952* (CXK-48673-CK-52867) and *The Voice—The Columbia Years* (C4K-40343-CK-40631)

A nearly flawless interpretation by Sinatra of a song he had been singing in concert and on radio for more than a year. Here he conveys the wonder of love with a gentle but absolute conviction.

Richard Whiting wrote the lyric for his wife, Eleanor, in 1928. A song that encompasses great warmth and sensitivity, it has remained a favorite throughout the years, immune to the changing values of generations of listeners.

An additional chorus sung for this particular recording is not included on either the November 21, 1943, recording from a *Songs by Sinatra* radio program dress rehearsal, available on *Frank Sinatra—The V-Discs* (C2K-66135-CK-66136), or on the March 2, 1960, recording at Capitol, available on *Nice 'n' Easy* (CDP 7-96827-2). The extra chorus was recorded for the movie *Meet Danny Wilson* on June 13, 1951, but it was edited from the master and subsequently not included in the film.

7

"If I Loved You"

Words by Oscar Hammerstein II and music by Richard
   Rodgers
Recorded May 1, 1945, in Hollywood
Arranged by Axel Stordahl
CD: *Frank Sinatra—The Columbia Years 1943–1952* (CXK-
   48673-CK-52867)

A glorious number from the Broadway musical *Carousel*—
and a quintessential moment for Sinatra and his arranger,
Axel Stordahl. Sinatra's vocal evokes both longing and sex-
ual desire. The Stordahl arrangement is superb, a chart that
succeeds in maximizing the effect of Sinatra's vocal work.

The song is one of Rodgers and Hammerstein's finest
anthems of love, and each revival of *Carousel* brings a
greater appreciation of its marvelous score.

Sinatra performed the song on radio, television, and in
concert throughout the 1940s and 1950s. On August 16,
1955, he recorded the song for the film version of *Carousel*.
An exquisite reading by Sinatra of a rarely sung verse and
a masterful arrangement by Nelson Riddle combine to
make for a stellar track. However, Sinatra subsequently
dropped out of the project and, with the exception of an
unauthorized release, the recording has never been issued.

8

``These Foolish Things''

Words by Holt Marvell and music by Jack Strachey and
  Harry Link
Recorded July 30, 1945, in Hollywood
Arranged by Axel Stordahl
CD: *Frank Sinatra—The Columbia Years 1943–1952* (CXK-
  48673-CK-52868) and *Frank Sinatra: The Voice—The Co-
  lumbia Years* (C4K-40343-CK-40634)

Sinatra, the great storyteller, in singing this song of lost
love and remembering in the summer of 1945, triumphs
in defining a time and place in a little more than three
minutes. Holt Marvell's lyrics are a melancholy expression
of bittersweet moments and terrible regret.

Spread It Abroad is a long-forgotten musical from 1935
with one memorable moment—''These Foolish Things.''
The song resurfaced six years later in the film *A Yank in the
RAF*. The myriad of choruses in the song has permitted a
great variety of interpretations by a great many recording
artists—from Nat King Cole to Ella Fitzgerald. Sinatra's
own final chorus on this recording is a prime example.

Sinatra recorded the song again on September 12, 1961,
for Capitol. The track is available on *Point of No Return* (CDP
7-48334-2).

*F*rank Sinatra was reunited with his mentor, Tommy Dorsey, when Dorsey appeared on the *Songs by Sinatra* radio program on October 24, 1945. Sinatra performed "I'll Never Smile Again" with the Pied Pipers, then he sang "Without a Song." Dress rehearsal versions of these performances are available on *Frank Sinatra—The V-Discs* (C2K-66135-CK-66137).

9

"The Song Is You"

Words by Oscar Hammerstein II and music by Jerome Kern
Recorded March 10, 1946, in Hollywood
Arranged by Axel Stordahl
CD: *Frank Sinatra—The Columbia Years 1943–1952* (CXK-48673-CK-52869)

Sinatra loved "The Song Is You" as much as he loved recording it. There is a dramatic dichotomy in his readings of the song: the soft ballad versions from the 1940s and the swinging renditions that materialized as Sinatra matured as an artist. This recording draws on the strength of the sublime ballad interpretation by Sinatra and the gorgeous string arrangement by Axel Stordahl. Although Sinatra would record the song again at both Capitol and Reprise—to great up-tempo arrangements by Billy May—

the nod goes to the Columbia ballad. It is simply a beautiful recording.

The song was written in 1932 for the Broadway musical *Music in the Air*. The show flopped, but the tune endured to become an American classic.

Sinatra recorded "The Song Is You" nine times. His first recording was made on January 19, 1942, available on *The Song Is You* (RCA 07863-66353-2); this CD also includes a recording of the song taken from a September 3, 1942, radio aircheck. A V-Disc recording from an *Old Gold* dress rehearsal, available on *Frank Sinatra—The V-Discs* (C2K-66135-CK-66137), was recorded on February 13, 1946. A second recording of the song for Columbia was done on October 26, 1947, available on *Frank Sinatra—The Columbia Years 1943–1952* (CXK-48673-CK-52869) and on *The Voice—The Columbia Years* (C4K-40343-CK-40631). For Capitol, Sinatra recorded the song on December 9, 1958, available on *Come Dance with Me* (CDP 7-48468-2) and *Frank Sinatra—The Capitol Years* (C2-94777). A recording at Reprise, from September 18, 1979, appears on *Trilogy: The Past* (Rep. CD 2300-2) and on *The Reprise Collection* (Rep. CD 9-26340-2). Two unissued recordings were made: one for Capitol on September 30, 1958, the other for Reprise on July 17, 1979.

Sinatra performed "The Song Is You" throughout most of his career.

*S*inatra performed "The Song Is You" countless times, but one performance stands out. Many critics consider his rendition of the song in concert at the Hollywood Bowl on August 14, 1943, to be the quintessential interpretation of the tune by Sinatra.

10

"Time After Time"

Words by Sammy Cahn and music by Jule Styne
Recorded October 24, 1946, in Hollywood
Arranged by Axel Stordahl
CD: *Frank Sinatra—The Columbia Years 1943–1952* (CXK 48673-CK-52870) and *The Voice—The Columbia Years* (C4K-40343-CK-40634)

A warmly passionate reading by Sinatra and a virtually flawless vocal performance. Axel Stordahl's orchestration perfectly complements the marvelous breath control and impeccable phrasing of the singer.

A high point in the collaborative work of Styne and Cahn, this ballad was written for the film *It Happened in Brooklyn*, starring Frank Sinatra.

In seven takes, Sinatra recorded the song for the film at MGM Studios on September 17, 1946. He recorded it again for Capitol Records on November 25, 1957. The track is available on a double CD: *Sinatra 80th—All the Best* (CDP 7243-8-35952-2).

Sinatra sang a delightful parody of the song at the Villa Capri in Hollywood on his forty-second birthday, December 12, 1957. The special lyrics provided by Sammy Cahn were a clever combination of humor and sentimentality.

11

``Always''

Words and music by Irving Berlin
Recorded January 9, 1947, in Hollywood
Arranged by Axel Stordahl
CD: *Frank Sinatra—The Columbia Years 1943–1952* CXK-48673-CK-52871) and *Hello Young Lovers* (CGK-40897: alternate take)

Sinatra's recording of ``Always'' on December 15, 1946, was undistinguished. In a little over three weeks, he went back into the studio with a new arrangement by Axel Stordahl to make what may be the consummate ballad recording of this Berlin classic.

Russian immigrant Irving Berlin became America's greatest songwriter—and its most successful. His versatility was unparalleled. Berlin composed the most sophisticated of Broadway melodies, great songs of patriotism, perennial holiday favorites, clever jingles, and beautiful ballads of rare simplicity and simple truths. This song belongs to the latter category.

A terrific swing version of the song, with a driving Nelson Riddle arrangement, was recorded by Sinatra for Capitol on August 23, 1960. It appears on Sinatra's *Swingin' Session! and More* (CDP 7-46573-2). Sinatra's original December 15, 1946 recording of the song is included on *Frank Sinatra—The Columbia Years 1943–1952* (CXK-48673-CK-52871).

A favorite Sinatra track from a few of Frank's friends:

Larry King: "There Used to Be a Ballpark" (1973)
Jerry Lewis: "All or Nothing at All" (1966)
Robert Wagner: "One for My Baby" (1958)
George Burns: "Young at Heart" (1953)
Tony Bennett: "Weep They Will" (1955)
Gregory Peck: "Let Me Try Again" (1973)
Bob Newhart: "The Way You Look Tonight" (1964)
Don Rickles: "My Way" (1968)

12

"But Beautiful"

Words by Johnny Burke and music by James Van Heusen
Recorded August 17, 1947, in Hollywood
Arranged by Axel Stordahl
CD: *Frank Sinatra—The Columbia Years 1943–1952* (CXK-48673-CK-52872) and *The Voice—The Columbia Years* (C4K-40343-CK-40634)

A hit song for Bing Crosby—but a bigger hit for Sinatra. Although "But Beautiful" is more readily identified with Crosby, Sinatra's version was a greater commercial success. This is not surprising, given Sinatra's genius at interpreting a truly great lyric, particularly a song that explores the nuances of love and romance.

One of the most successful songwriting teams of the 1940s, Johnny Burke and James Van Heusen wrote many of Crosby's biggest hits, including this gem in 1947. They would eventually write songs for sixteen Crosby films, including an Academy Award winner, "Swinging on a Star," for the classic film *Going My Way*.

Sinatra and Van Heusen, who wrote some of Sinatra's biggest hits, were friends for over forty years. Sinatra called him Chester. Johnny Burke, the brilliant lyricist whom Sinatra dubbed the Poet, began his songwriting career in 1926 after landing a job as a piano salesman for Irving Berlin Inc., New York.

Inexplicably, Sinatra rarely performed the song. There were only a handful of radio and TV performances, and a few concert performances in the mid-1970s.

13

"Night and Day"

Words and Music by Cole Porter
Recorded October 22, 1947, in New York City
Arranged by Axel Stordahl
CD: *Frank Sinatra—The Columbia Years 1943–1952* (CXK-48673-CK-52872)

A magnificent recording mysteriously abandoned and discovered forty-six years later. Why had the song been discarded? At the recording session, Sinatra inquired about the running time of the song—three minutes and thirty-nine seconds. Therein may lie the answer: perhaps Sinatra thought the song was too long to be commercially viable.

From 1945 through 1947, Sinatra opened his weekly radio show with "Night and Day." For the singer, the song would become an evergreen. Over the next four decades, he would perform it in a vast array of interpretations. It has received full orchestral treatments as a ballad and as an up-tempo number. It has been sung with just guitar, with the verse in the middle, with bongo and flute, with a vibraphone, and with a variety of small jazz arrangements.

The Cole Porter song was written in 1932 for Fred Astaire for the musical *The Gay Divorce*, renamed *The Gay*

Divorcée for the 1934 film version. The impact of the song was so great that people began referring to the musical as the *Night and Day Show*.

Raised on a farm in the Midwest, Cole Porter became the epitome of urbane wit and sophistication. He wrote more than eight hundred songs. An amazing percentage went on to become great standards—but perhaps none more so than "Night and Day."

Sinatra recorded the song at his first solo session on January 19, 1942. It is available on *The Song Is You* (RCA 07863-66353-2). A definitive swing version with arranger Nelson Riddle was recorded on November 26, 1956, at Capitol Records, available on *A Swingin' Affair!* (CDP 7-94518-2), on *Frank Sinatra Sings the Select Cole Porter* (CDP 7-96611-2), and on *Frank Sinatra—The Capitol Years* (C2-94777).

Another version, this one with the verse, was recorded for Reprise on November 22, 1961, It is available on *Sinatra and Strings* (Rep. CD 9-27020-2), on *A Man and His Music* (Rep. CD 1016-2), and on *The Reprise Collection* (Rep. CD 9-26340-2). A memorable live recording at the Olympia in Paris on June 5, 1962, shows up on *Sinatra and Sextet: Live in Paris* (Rep. CD 9-45487-2); this ballad version, with the verse accompanied by Al Viola on solo guitar, features an exquisite reading by Sinatra. Finally, there's an ill-advised disco recording from February 16, 1977, included on *The Complete Sinatra* (Rep. CD 46013-2), a twenty-CD collection from Reprise.

*M*any music critics have likened the cadence and tone of Sinatra's voice to that of a trombone. The fact that Tommy Dorsey played the trombone is not a co-incidence. It was during his years with Dorsey that Sinatra learned breath control, in particular "circular" breathing. From listening to Dorsey play, Sinatra learned the use of dynamics. He also copied Dorsey's legato style, which he used to maximum effect in his interpretation of ballads.

14

"Fools Rush In"

Words by Johnny Mercer and music by Rube Bloom
Recorded October 31, 1947, in New York City
Arranged by Axel Stordahl
CD: *Frank Sinatra—The Columbia Years 1943–1952* (CXK-48673-CK-52873)

An incredible vocal by Sinatra in which he seems to crawl inside the lyric to convey all that the author intended. Stordahl's arrangement is perfectly restrained to heighten the vocal performance. Sinatra's breath control is extraordinary.

A Tin Pan Alley tune written in 1940, "Fools Rush In" was taken to the top spot on the *Hit Parade* by Glenn Miller and His Orchestra. Johnny Mercer's lyric begins with a line from seventeenth-century English poet and satirist Alexander Pope: "Fools rush in where angels fear to tread." The opening verse has been often omitted by Sinatra—but he includes it here.

Sinatra first recorded the song on March 29, 1940, with Tommy Dorsey, available on *The Song Is You* (RCA 07863-66353-2). A more resigned interpretation by Sinatra was done for Capitol on March 1, 1960. It appears on *Nice 'n' Easy* (CDP 7-96827-2).

---

*T*here were certain songs that Sinatra had difficulty remembering—so he rarely performed them in concert. "Fools Rush In" and "You Go to My Head" are two prime examples. During his appearances in the mid-1950s at the Copa in New York City, Sinatra would enlist the help of a waiter before going on stage. In his dressing room, Sinatra would sing the song to the waiter, who would verify each word against the sheet music.

15

"Body and Soul"

Words by Edward Heyman, Robert Sour, Frank Eyton, and
  music by Johnny Green
Recorded November 9, 1947, in New York City
Arranged by Axel Stordahl
CD: *Frank Sinatra—The Columbia Years 1943–1952* (CXK-
  48673-CK-52873) and *The Voice—The Columbia Years*
  (C4K-40343-CK-40634: alternate take)

Sinatra's vocal soars on the wings of an ethereal arrangement by Axel Stordahl and a heavenly trumpet solo by the
great Bobby Hackett. Sinatra is not identified with "Body
and Soul" and rarely performed it—but his magnificent
recording of it in the fall of 1947 warrants its inclusion
here.

Written in 1930 for the play *Three's a Crowd*, starring
Clifton Webb, Libby Holman, and Fred Allen, this song was
an immediate sensation and became one of the most popular songs of all time, covered by practically every major
jazz and pop artist.

Thirty-seven years after the Columbia session, Sinatra
returned to this masterpiece. He recorded it on April 13,
1984, to a terrific jazz chart by Bob James, in a session
conducted by Quincy Jones. But Sinatra was not comfort-
able with the results, and it has never been released.

*A*l Viola, Sinatra's guitarist for over twenty years, provided *Sinatra 101* with his fifteen all-time favorite Sinatra recordings:

1. "The House I Live In"
2. "All the Way"
3. "One for My Baby"
4. "Guess I'll Hang My Tears Out to Dry"
5. "Angel Eyes"
6. "All or Nothing at All"
7. "Night and Day"
8. "Violets for Your Furs"
9. "My Funny Valentine"
10. "In the Wee Small Hours"
11. "I've Got You Under My Skin"
12. "I Get a Kick Out of You"
13. "On a Clear Day"
14. "You're Nobody 'til Somebody Loves You"
15. "Goody Goody"

16

``Lover''

Words by Lorenz Hart and music by Richard Rodgers
Recorded April 14, 1950, in New York City
Arranged by George Siravo
CD: *Frank Sinatra—The Columbia Years 1943–1952* (CXK-48673-CK-52876)

In April 1950, Sinatra was on the skids. His records weren't selling. He had lost his film contract. He was experiencing vocal problems. He was desperately in need of a new direction.

He found it in the wonderful swing arrangements of George Siravo. The legendary sessions in the spring of 1950 produced Sinatra's first great ten-inch LP. It also unveiled Sinatra the swinger—a style that Sinatra would sharpen and perfect in the 1950s.

``Lover'' is a daring vocal by Sinatra. He reaches for notes that seriously challenge his abilities—but the resulting sound is electrifying. Siravo's bold arrangement—a foreshadowing of the arrangements to come from Nelson Riddle—cleverly involve the augmentation of each individual musical instrument. Ken Lane's piano solo on this track is a prime example.

This particular recording uses a vocal overdub. Sinatra was in such fragile voice during the recording session that producer Mitch Miller turned off the singer's microphone.

The actual vocals were taped a few weeks later, in the small hours of the morning.

"Lover" was composed in 1932 for the film *Love Me To-night*, starring Jeanette MacDonald and Maurice Chevalier. The composers, Rodgers and Hart, had just returned to Hollywood after a major flop on Broadway, *The Hot Heiress.* Ironically, another song from the film was picked as the big hit: "Mimi." But the following year, "Lover" hit the charts and went on to become an American pop standard.

Sinatra recorded the song once more, at Capitol on March 22, 1961. Although wonderfully done, it lacks the fire and daring of the 1950 session. It is available on *Come Swing with Me* (CDP 7-94520-2).

17

"Nevertheless"

Words by Bert Kalmar and music by Harry Ruby
Recorded October 9, 1950, in New York City
Arranged by George Siravo
CD: *Frank Sinatra—The Columbia Years 1943–1952* (CXK-48673-CK-52876) and *The Voice—The Columbia Years* (C4K-40343-CK-40631)

A troubling time for Sinatra—and a great moment for American popular music. Here art imitates life. At the crossroads of a broken marriage and the uncertainty of a new relationship, the singer makes a strong personal statement. He is hopelessly in love—and the consequences do not seem to matter. An outstanding trumpet solo by Billy Butterfield works to isolate the resignation that Sinatra brings to the song.

Written in 1931, "Nevertheless" had been around for almost twenty years before the Mills Brothers turned it into a huge hit. An introspective work on the perils of romantic commitment, the song never fully achieved the success it deserved. Sinatra recorded "Nevertheless" at Capitol on March 2, 1960. Available on *Nice 'n' Easy* (CDP 7-96827-2), it showcases a more self-assured singer, backed by a lush Nelson Riddle arrangement.

"*T*hese are just a few of the many songs that I love," said Sid Mark. The host of *The Sounds of Sinatra*, a nationally syndicated radio program, picked his twenty-five all-time favorite Sinatra recordings for *Sinatra 101*. They are arranged chronologically.

"I Fall in Love Too Easily" (1944)
"Why Try to Change Me Now?" (1952)
"I'm a Fool to Want You" (1957)
"So Long, My Love" (1957)
"Guess I'll Hang My Tears Out to Dry" (1958)
"Here's That Rainy Day" (1959)
"Embraceable You" (1960)
"Come Rain or Come Shine" (1961)
"Pennies from Heaven" (1962)
"California" (1963)
"I Have Dreamed" (1963)
"Golden Moment" (1965)

"I'll Only Miss Her When I Think of Her" (1965)
"September of My Years" (1965)
"Change Partners" (1967)
"Drinking Again" (1967)
"How Insensitive" (1967)
"Younger Than Springtime" (1967)
"All My Tomorrows" (1969)
"Elizabeth" (1969)
"Forget to Remember" (1969)
"Just as Though You Were Here" (1974)
"What Are You Doing the Rest of Your Life?"
    (1974)
"MacArthur Park" (1979)
"You and Me" (1979)

18

"I'm a Fool to Want You"

Words by Jack Wolf and Frank Sinatra, music by Joel S.
   Herron
Recorded March 27, 1951, in New York City
Arranged by Axel Stordahl
CD: *Frank Sinatra—The Columbia Years 1943–1952* (CXK-
   48673-CK-52877) and *The Voice—The Columbia Years*
   (C4K-40343-CK-40632)

A painful moment for Sinatra, but a giant leap for his in-
terpretive genius. Here, Sinatra sings with his heart on his
sleeve. His performance is a cry from the soul. Music critic
George Simon called this particular track the most emotional recording ever made by Frank Sinatra.

Ben Barton, the head of Sinatra's music publishing company, acquired the song for the singer. Sinatra rewrote
some of the lyrics—to the extent that he was given credit
with Jack Wolf as co-lyricist. Outside of the Sinatra world,
the song has remained relatively obscure.

Sinatra recorded the song for Capitol on May 1, 1957,
to a thoughtful arrangement by Gordon Jenkins. It is available on *Where Are You?* (CDP 7-91209-2) and on *Frank
Sinatra—The Capitol Years* (C2-94777 CDP 7-94319-2).
Although Sinatra gives an absolutely beautiful reading, it
lacks the raw emotional anguish of the 1951 recording.

19

"The Birth of the Blues"

Words by Buddy De Sylva and Lew Brown, music by Ray
   Henderson
Recorded June 3, 1952, in Hollywood
Arranged by Heinie Beau
CD: *Frank Sinatra—The Columbia Years 1943–1952* (CXK-
   48673-CK-52877) and *The Voice—The Columbia Years*
   (C4K-40343-CK-40633)

"The Birth of the Blues" may be the first great recording
of the mature Sinatra. Certainly it was a harbinger of things
to come. On this track, Sinatra employs a rough guttural
sound that he would call upon in the 1950s to "punch up"
his swing tunes. The technique would serve Sinatra well
for more than four decades.

The song was recorded using a chart written by Heinie
Beau. Axel Stordahl conducted the studio orchestra.

Harry Richman introduced the song in *George White's
Scandals* in 1926. Paul Whiteman and His Orchestra enjoyed a huge hit with it the same year. Over the years, it
has become a great standard.

A memorable moment in entertainment history occurred on TV's *The Edsel Show* on October 13, 1957, when Sinatra teamed with Louis Armstrong to sing "The Birth of the Blues."

20

"Why Try to Change Me Now?"

Words by Joseph McCarthy and music by Cy Coleman
Recorded September 17, 1952, in New York City
Arranged by Percy Faith
CD: *Frank Sinatra—The Columbia Years 1943–1952* (CXK-48673-CK-52877) and *The Voice—The Columbia Years* (C4K-40343-CK-40634)

Sinatra's last recording for Columbia Records—and an appropriate song in the context of his life. Gone was the innocent, naive singer of the previous decade. Burned by love, the singer is able to convey the darkness, the sadness, and the cynicism that would characterize much of his work in the years to come.

A melancholy tune composed by a young Cy Coleman, "Why Try to Change Me Now?" never created much of a ripple in its time. It is best remembered as simply "a Sinatra song."

In a more somber reading, Sinatra recorded the song at Capitol on March 24, 1959. In his phrasing of the word "clown," Sinatra created an ineffable moment that effectively captures the loss and sorrow that are at the core of the song. Arranged by Gordon Jenkins, the recording appears on *No One Cares* (CDP 7-94519-2).

Sinatra did an exquisite recording of this song with Harry Sosnick and His Orchestra for the *Treasury Department's Guest Star* radio program. The actual recording date is unknown, but the show was aired on May 3, 1953. The track is available only on an unauthorized release.

THE
CAPITOL
YEARS

21

``I've Got the World on a String''

Words by Ted Koehler and music by Harold Arlen
Recorded April 30, 1953, in Los Angeles
Arranged by Nelson Riddle
CD: *Frank Sinatra— The Capitol Collector's Series* (CDP 7-
   92160-2) and *Frank Sinatra—The Capitol Years* (C2-94777
   CDP 7-94318-2)

The beginning of the remarkable alliance between Sinatra, thirty-seven, and arranger-conductor Nelson Riddle, thirty-one. They would work in tandem for the next quarter century, creating a body of work unparalleled in American popular music in terms of beauty, intelligence, and staying power.

This, their first collaborative effort, is definitive. In concert, the song was one of Sinatra's favorite openings, and always with the Riddle arrangement. The sound of a Riddle chart is instantly recognizable. His work was brilliant—and his contribution to Sinatra's career is immeasurable.

Composers Ted Koehler and Harold Arlen wrote the song in 1932 for the Cotton Club in Harlem. Arlen also composed for stage shows, including *Earl Carroll Vanities*, which introduced the song to a larger audience.

Sinatra recorded the song again on July 1, 1993, for *Duets* (CDP 0777-7-89611-2) with the Riddle arrangement.

22

``Don't Worry 'bout Me''

Words by Ted Koehler and music by Rube Bloom
Recorded April 30, 1953, in Los Angeles
Arranged by Nelson Riddle
CD: *Frank Sinatra—The Collector's Series* (CDP 7-92160-2)
   and *Where Are You?* (CDP 7-91209-2)

Sinatra's second recording with Riddle would be as memorable as the first. Another Ted Koehler lyric is given the full treatment by the arranger and singer—as Riddle's arrangement perfectly complements Sinatra's vocal. The world-weary sound from Sinatra would become his trademark technique for dark ballads over the next forty-plus years.

Not long after the session, Sinatra performed the song in concert. The stage performance would contain the verse. There is no known studio recording of it.

The song was introduced by Cab Calloway in the revue *Cotton Club Parade* at the Harlem club in 1939. That same year, the tune was a hit for Hal Kemp and His Orchestra.

A jazzier version by Sinatra is available on *Sinatra at the Sands* (Rep. CD 1019-2), with Count Basie and His Orchestra. Reprise recorded a number of Sinatra shows at the Sands between January 26 and February 1, 1966. The best performances were compiled for the album release.

*O*n April 30, 1953, Sinatra was elated by the sound that arranger Nelson Riddle had created for him. During the playbacks that evening, Sinatra made the rounds in the studio, gleefully slapping the backs of musicians and technicians, and telling many of them that he was back.

23

"My One and Only Love"

Words by Robert Mellin and music by Guy Wood
Recorded May 2, 1953, in Los Angeles
Arranged by Nelson Riddle
CD: *Nice 'n' Easy* (CDP 7-96827-2)

A clinic by Sinatra on the art of singing a lush romantic ballad—in his third recording session with Riddle. Seven months shy of his thirty-eighth birthday, Sinatra still possessed the skills from his early years as a crooner, but now with the ability to interpret with greater depth and feeling. Certainly the Riddle sound played a big part. It gave Sinatra a larger canvas for artistic expression, and it enabled him to discover the mature artist within.

The greatness of Sinatra's gifts as a singer are evident on this track. The exquisite phrasing, extended passages and incredible range provide a clinic for any would-be singer.

This relatively obscure ballad, written by Robert Mellin and Guy Wood in 1953, is a worthy discovery.

24

``A Foggy Day''

Words by Ira Gershwin and music by George Gershwin
Recorded November 5, 1953, in Los Angeles
Arranged by Nelson Riddle and George Siravo
CD: *Songs for Young Lovers and Swing Easy* (CDP 7-48470-2)

The first recording for the first concept album. Many music critics, including Stephen Holden of *The New York Times*, consider Sinatra a pioneer in this art form. Not just a random compilation of songs on a slab of vinyl, the eight songs on *Songs for Young Lovers* collectively tell a story.

Composed by Ira and George Gershwin, ``A Foggy Day'' was introduced by Fred Astaire in the 1937 film *A Damsel in Distress*. A smart and sophisticated tribute to London, it is as fresh and witty today as six decades ago, a testimony to the timelessness of the Gershwins.

Sinatra would perform the song for more than forty years. A second recording was done on December 19, 1960, with a Johnny Mandel arrangement, for Sinatra's first Reprise album, *Ring-a-Ding-Ding* (Rep. CD 9-27017-2). A third recording was done with the Mandel arrangement on October 12, 1993 for Capitol's *Duets II* (CDP 7243-8-

28103-2). A concert performance from June 5, 1962, is available on *Sinatra and Sextet: Live in Paris* (Rep. CD 9-45487-2).

---

*D*ebate about whether Nelson Riddle or George Siravo charted the musical arrangements for the album *Songs for Young Lovers* has persisted for many years. Credit was originally given to Riddle—but many believed that Siravo's contributions deserved to be acknowledged. One theory is that Siravo charted the songs for small-combo arrangements—his specialty—and that his arrangements were subsequently rewritten for adaptation for a larger orchestra by Riddle. In an interview in 1984, a year before his death, Riddle called the musical arrangements for the work a "hybrid" of himself and Siravo. Nevertheless, Capitol now credits only Siravo. For the purposes of *Sinatra 101*, the authors have credited both arrangers.

25

``My Funny Valentine''

Words by Lorenz Hart and music by Richard Rodgers
Recorded November 5, 1953, in Los Angeles
Arranged by Nelson Riddle and George Siravo
CD: *Songs for Young Lovers and Swing Easy* (CDP 7-48470-2)
    and *Frank Sinatra Sings the Select Rodgers and Hart* (CDP
    0777-7-80323-2)

A masterpiece from Sinatra and Riddle. It is the version by which all other interpretations, before or since, are invariably measured. Sinatra's warm, intimate vocal and Riddle's beautifully understated arrangement combine for a great moment in the history of American pop music.

The lyric is a remarkable work from Lorenz Hart. A New York drama critic, in a review of Shakespeare in the Park, extolled Shakespeare as the greatest poet in the history of the English language—with the exception of Lorenz Hart. Who but Lorenz Hart could successfully write a song of romantic love extolling the virtues of imperfection as the ideal object of affection? The song was composed for the Broadway musical *Babes in Arms* in 1937, sung by Mitzi Green.

The song would become a Sinatra staple in concert for the next forty years. In the latter part of his career, Sinatra would add a lovely coda that worked to effectively augment the warm sentiment of the tune.

44

On October 14, 1993, Sinatra recorded the song again, for *Duets II* (CDP 7243-8-28103-2). In a wistful pairing with Lorrie Morgan, Sinatra sings "My Funny Valentine," in an arrangement by Patrick Williams, while Morgan sings "How Do You Keep the Music Playing?," a haunting ballad written by Michel Legrand with lyrics by Alan and Marilyn Bergman. A live performance of "My Funny Valentine," from 1962, appears on *Sinatra and Sextet: Live in Paris* (Rep. CD 9-45487-2).

26

"They Can't Take That Away from Me"

Words by Ira Gershwin and music by George Gershwin
Recorded November 3, 1953, in Los Angeles
Arranged by Nelson Riddle and George Siravo
CD: *Songs for Young Lovers and Swing Easy* (CDP 7-48470-2)
   and *Frank Sinatra—The Capitol Years* (C2-94777 CDP 7-94318-2)

Sinatra begins to overtly reshape the material he is singing. With his personality becoming increasingly integral to the song itself, Sinatra finds himself altering the composer's original concept for a tune. "They Can't Take That Away from Me" is a prime example. Here Sinatra takes a classic ballad, and with a jazzy Riddle touch, transforms the song into a lilting up-tempo piece. The metamorphosis of traditional pop standards to fit the Sinatra persona would increasingly become a Sinatra trademark.

The song was composed by the Gershwins for the 1937 film *Shall We Dance?*, and introduced by Fred Astaire. The great Astaire would reprise the song in his final film with Ginger Rogers, *The Barkleys of Broadway*, in 1949.

In a span of thirty years, Sinatra recorded the song at three different sessions. There would be a combined total of twelve takes, including false starts. The second recording was for Reprise on April 10, 1962, for *Sinatra and Swingin' Brass* (Rep. CD 9-27021-2). This track, arranged by Neal Hefti, is virtually on a par with the Capitol classic. It is also available on *My Kind of Broadway* (Rep. CD 1015-2). On July 1, 1993, Sinatra recorded the song again for Capitol's *Duets* (CDP 0777-7-89611-2) in an arrangement written by Patrick Williams. A live track is available on *Sinatra and Sextet: Live in Paris* (Rep. CD 9-45487-2), recorded on June 5, 1962.

---

*S*inatra guitarist and arranger Tony Mottola shared with *Sinatra 101* his fifteen all-time favorite Sinatra albums:

1. *Sinatra and Strings*
2. *September of My Years*
3. *The Concert Sinatra*
4. *Sinatra and Jobim*
5. *Sinatra and Basie*
6. *In the Wee Small Hours*
7. *Songs for Swingin' Lovers*
8. *Come Fly with Me*
9. *A Man and His Music*

10. *Ol' Blue Eyes Is Back*
11. *Sinatra and Ellington*
12. *Point of No Return*
13. *She Shot Me Down*
14. *Nice 'n' Easy*
15. *For Only the Lonely*

27

"Like Someone in Love"

Words by Johnny Burke and music by James Van Heusen
Recorded November 6, 1953, in Los Angeles
Arranged by Nelson Riddle and George Siravo
CD: *Songs for Young Lovers and Swing Easy* (CDP 7-48470-2)

A song Sinatra promised Johnny Burke he would record someday. Fortunately, he kept his word. A glorious recording by Sinatra, the session was taped nearly eight and a half years after Sinatra had first performed the song on his radio show in the spring of 1945.

The track is particularly notable for the way Sinatra brings to each line an element of amazement, not unlike the wonder of falling in love. A subdued orchestral chart enhances the romantic motif.

Dinah Shore introduced the song in 1944, in a forgettable musical film, *The Belle of the Yukon*. Bing Crosby scored a minor hit with the song in 1945.

28

``I Get a Kick Out of You''

Words and music by Cole Porter
Recorded November 6, 1953, in Los Angeles
Arranged by Nelson Riddle and George Siravo
CD: *Songs for Young Lovers and Swing Easy* (CDP 7-48470-2)
   and *Frank Sinatra—The Capitol Years* (C2-94777 CDP 7-94318-2)

Sinatra's affinity for sophistication and cynicism endowed him with the ability to interpret the songs of Cole Porter better than any of his contemporaries. His interpretation of Porter material is part of his legend. Of the many songs Sinatra recorded by Cole Porter, perhaps none is more definitive than "I Get a Kick Out of You."

The song has been recorded by practically every major artist since November 21, 1934. That's when Ethel Merman introduced the song at the Alvin Theater in the Broadway musical *Anything Goes*.

For Sinatra, the song was always a personal statement, stemming from the public perception that he digs all those people who adore him. He could never seem to sing the song badly. His first crack at it was in the summer of 1943, a plush ballad version with the Bobby Tucker Singers that aired on the radio show *Broadway Bandbox*. For the Capitol session of 1953, the verse to the song was added.

He recorded the song again (minus the verse) on April 10, 1962, to a stellar arrangement by Neal Hefti. This version is available on *Sinatra and Swingin' Brass* (Rep. CD 9-27021-2) and on *The Reprise Collection* (Rep. CD 9-26340-2). An unreleased track was recorded for Capitol's *Duets* project on July 1, 1993.

Two live recordings are also available. *Sinatra and Sextet: Live in Paris* (Rep. CD 9-45487-2), recorded in 1962, is particularly outstanding. The song also appears on *Sinatra/The Main Event—Live* (Rep. CD 2207-2). This recording, from a concert at New York's Madison Square Garden on October 13, 1974, is intercut with a verse performed at the Spectrum in Philadelphia six days earlier.

29

"Little Girl Blue"

Words by Lorenz Hart and music by Richard Rodgers
Recorded November 6, 1953, in Los Angeles
Arranged by Nelson Riddle and George Siravo
CD: *Songs for Young Lovers and Swing Easy* (CDP 7-48470-2)
  and *Frank Sinatra Sings the Select Rodgers and Hart* (CDP 0777-7-80323-2)

An incredibly sensitive reading by Sinatra of a song he had already perfected in concert. Sinatra's strong vocal, backed by an exquisite orchestral arrangement, brings a contemplative quality to the recording. The verse by Lorenz Hart is arguably his best. Sinatra's reading of it is nonpareil. Riddle deftly backs Sinatra as he captures the pathos of Hart's finely honed poetic expressions.

This Rodgers and Hart song was written for Billy Rose's 1935 production of *Jumbo,* and introduced by Gloria Grafton. A recording of it by Margaret Whiting made the charts in 1947.

Sinatra resurrected the song in the early 1980s. A concert version, accompanied only by Tony Mottola on guitar, is outstanding for its simplicity and beauty. A commercial recording does not exist.

---

*N*elson Riddle was asked in 1984 to name his favorite Capitol project with Frank Sinatra. His response: "I would have to say *Swing Easy.* It was the most inventive and most exciting work we did together."

30

``Day In, Day Out''

Words by Johnny Mercer and music by Rube Bloom
Recorded March 1, 1954, in Los Angeles
Arranged by Nelson Riddle
CD: *Nice 'n' Easy* (CDP 7-96827-2)

One of three great recordings of the song by Sinatra, each with a different arranger. This second recording—the second of two obscure ballad versions—reaps the benefit of Sinatra having a better handle on it. He had been performing the ballad version for more than a year.

The recording, arranged by Nelson Riddle, had languished for more than three decades, available only on a rare EP and foreign-issue LP. Its inclusion as a "bonus track" on the *Nice 'n' Easy* CD brought it to the mass market.

The original recording, commercially undiscovered until the early 1990s, was cut on April 2, 1953. Nicely arranged by Axel Stordahl, the song appears on *Point of No Return* (CDP 7-48334-2) and on *Frank Sinatra Sings the Select Johnny Mercer* (CDP 0777-7-80326-2). Between the two ballad recordings is an extraordinary live performance—as a ballad—performed by Sinatra in London for the BBC *Showband Show* on July 16, 1953. An unauthorized recording is available on CD.

The third recording, for the album *Come Dance with Me*

(CDP 7-48468-2), was taped on December 22, 1958. Brilliantly arranged by Billy May, it is a rousing swing interpretation. This marvelous track is also available on *Frank Sinatra Sings the Select Johnny Mercer* (CDP 0777-7-80326-2). Another swing recording from eleven days earlier remains commercially unavailable. A concert version of May's swing arrangement is available on *Sinatra and Sextet: Live in Paris* (Rep. CD 9-45487-2), recorded on June 5, 1962.

31

"Last Night When We Were Young"

Words by Yip Harburg and music by Harold Arlen
Recorded March 1, 1954, in Los Angeles
Arranged by Nelson Riddle
CD: *In the Wee Small Hours* (CDP 7-96826-2)

The first track recorded for the album *In the Wee Small Hours*—the beginning of Sinatra's greatest years as a recording artist. A sublime reading by Sinatra captures the bittersweet feeling of lost innocence and the morning after.

This great tune barely escaped obscurity. Lawrence Tibbett recorded the song for the 1935 film *Metropolitan*, but it was deleted in the final cut. In 1949, Judy Garland recorded it for the film *In the Good Old Summertime*, and again it was deleted.

On April 13, 1965, Sinatra recorded a new version of the song for the *September of My Years* album (Rep. CD 1014-

2), arranged by Gordon Jenkins. Sinatra delivers a credible reading, but his vocal is not as pure as on the original 1954 track. At Carnegie Hall on April 8, 1974, Reprise taped a recording of Sinatra singing the song as part of a saloon trilogy. It has never been released.

---

*T*ony Renaud, radio personality and personal friend of Barbara and Frank Sinatra, provided *Sinatra 101* with his top-ten list of Sinatra recordings:

1. "All My Tomorrows" (1969)
2. "I've Got You Under My Skin" (1956)
3. "The Lady Is a Tramp" (1956)
4. "Where or When" (1966)
5. "The Way You Look Tonight" (1964)
6. "Nice 'n' Easy" (1960)
7. "Summer Wind" (1966)
8. "You and Me" (1979)
9. "Oh, You Crazy Moon" (1965)
10. "Please Be Kind" (1962)

32

``Just One of Those Things''

Words and music by Cole Porter
Recorded April 7, 1954, in Los Angeles
Arranged by Nelson Riddle
CD: *Songs for Young Lovers and Swing Easy* (CDP 7-48470-2)
  and *Frank Sinatra Sings the Select Cole Porter*
  (CDP 7-96611-2)

The second of Sinatra's great concept albums is *Swing Easy*. The small and intimate jazz sound captures the atmosphere of a nightclub performance. Lots of experimentation pass between singer and arranger. Sinatra was taking more liberties with lyrics and Riddle was creating a new sound for both the singer and the song. It is the verbal and melodic improvisations of Sinatra and Riddle on ``Just One of Those Things'' that deliver a Cole Porter song from popularity to perfection.

Originally composed for the 1935 Broadway musical *Jubilee*, the song was introduced on stage by June Knight and Charles Walters.

Sinatra recorded the song again on July 13 and 14, 1954, for the film *Young at Heart*. It is a superb recording—but obscure—available only in LP format from Warner Bros. (*Fifty Years of Film Music*, WB3XX2736). Reprise recorded a live performance by Sinatra at the Sands Hotel in Las Vegas on November 5, 1961, but it remains unissued.

33

``All of Me''

Words by Seymour Simons and music by Gerald Marks
Recorded April 19, 1954, in Los Angeles
Arranged by Nelson Riddle
CD: *Songs for Young Lovers and Swing Easy* (CDP 7-48470-2)
   and *Frank Sinatra—The Capitol Years* (C2-94777 CDP 7-
   94318-2)

Sinatra had been singing ``All of Me'' for more than a
decade before entering the studio in the spring of 1954
to record this Riddle-orchestrated gem. Here Sinatra
gives a persuasive reading of a brief opus with imploring
lyrics.

Written in 1931, the song was originally performed on
radio by Belle Baker and in the same year it was in the
film *Careless Lady*. The following year, both Louis Armstrong and Paul Whiteman and His Orchestra scored
number-one hits with ``All of Me,'' one of the most recorded songs of the century.

Sinatra performed the song throughout his career—on
radio, television, and in concert—characteristically singing it with great zeal. He first recorded the song at a V-
Disc session on July 8, 1944, available on *Frank Sinatra—
The V-Discs* (C2K-66135-CK-66136). A pair of recordings
from the Columbia years were taped on November 6,
1946, and October 19, 1947; both are available on *Frank*

Sinatra—The Columbia Years 1943–1952 (CXK-48673-CK-52870 and CK-52872). On June 13, 1951, a recording was done for the film *Meet Danny Wilson*. Although never commercially released, it is available on an unauthorized CD.

---

*B*illy May, Gordon Jenkins, and Ernie Freeman each won a Grammy for best arrangement of a Sinatra chart. Nelson Riddle—Sinatra's greatest arranger—never received the same honor.

34

"Get Happy"

Words by Ted Koehler and music by Harold Arlen
Recorded April 19, 1954, in Los Angeles
Arranged by Nelson Riddle
CD: *Songs for Young Lovers and Swing Easy* (CDP 7-48470-2)

A bubbly confection written in the bleakness of the Great Depression, "Get Happy" would grow in popularity as the years passed. Here, the Sinatra-Riddle rendition has energy to burn. It is a jaunty romp in which Sinatra—and the driving jazz-swing beat of the band—impart a contagious message of joy.

"Get Happy" was the first song published by composer Harold Arlen, the son of a cantor from Buffalo, New York. At the time of publication, 1930, Arlen had been working in radio and theater as a rehearsal pianist. His first composition began as a rehearsal vamp. Ruth Etting introduced the song in the Broadway musical *9:15 Revue*.

The song would not become a Sinatra staple. He would sing it on television a few times, including a memorable *Colgate Comedy Hour* performance on November 29, 1953, joined by Harold Arlen on piano.

35

"Taking a Chance on Love"

Words by John Latouche and Ted Fetter, music by Vernon
   Duke, John Latouche, and Ted Fetter
Recorded April 19, 1954, in Los Angeles
Arranged by Nelson Riddle
CD: *Songs for Young Lovers and Swing Easy* (CDP 7-48470-2)
   and *Frank Sinatra—The Capitol Years* (C2-94777 CDP 7-
   94318-2)

An exhilarating vocal by Sinatra—the last track at the final recording session for the *Swing Easy* album. Here Sinatra exhibits an even greater command of a new style, a promise of things to come.

Ethel Waters introduced the song in the 1940 Broadway musical *Cabin in the Sky*, performing it again in the 1943 film version, in which Lena Horne also sang a chorus. That year, Benny Goodman and His Orchestra took the song to the top of the charts, where it remained for three consecutive weeks.

Sinatra performed the song on radio, television, and in concert. A jazz-oriented version was recorded for the *Perfectly Frank* radio series in midsummer of 1954. It was one of sixty-six studio recordings Sinatra would make for the series. The late jazz drummer Alvin Stoller noted that Sinatra would lay down twelve to fifteen tracks per session. Although there are no official releases from this series, many are available on unauthorized CDs.

36

``Someone to Watch Over Me''

Words by Ira Gershwin and music by George Gershwin
Recorded September 23, 1954, in Los Angeles
Arranged by Nelson Riddle
CD: *Nice 'n' Easy* (CDP 7-96827-2) and *Frank Sinatra—The Capitol Years* (C2-94777 CDP 7-94318-2)

An extraordinary vocal by Sinatra on a recording that for many years was difficult to obtain. Sinatra's sensitive reading makes for one of the most tender interpretations of this all-time classic. Nelson Riddle's arrangement is intelligent and discerning, perfectly augmenting the vocal without intrusion.

The song was introduced by Gertrude Lawrence in the 1926 Broadway musical *Oh, Kay*. The song title was suggested by composer Howard Dietz. The following year, the song became a smash hit.

Sinatra performed "Someone to Watch Over Me" for more than fifty years. His first recording of it was for a V-Disc on October 11, 1944, from a *Vimms Vitamins Show* dress rehearsal. It is available on *Frank Sinatra—The V-Discs* (C2K-66135-CK-66136). A recording was done for Columbia on July 30, 1945. This appears on *Frank Sinatra—The Columbia Years 1943–1952* (CXK-48673-CK-52868) and on *The Voice—The Columbia Years* (C4K-40343-CK-40631). An unreleased recording was done on the Warner Bros. sound stage on July 12, 1954, for the film *Young at Heart*.

---

*T*he music sheet from Warner Bros. for the film *Young at Heart* erroneously credits André Previn for the piano work on the song "Someone to Watch Over Me." The AFM (American Federation of Musicians) sheet shows that it was not Previn, but rather Sinatra's longtime pianist Bill Miller.

37

``Glad to Be Unhappy''

Words by Lorenz Hart and music by Richard Rodgers
Recorded February 8, 1955, in Los Angeles
Arranged by Nelson Riddle
CD: *In the Wee Small Hours* (CDP 7-96826-2) and *Frank Sinatra Sings the Select Rodgers and Hart* (CDP 0777-7-80323-2)

Sinatra's first concept album issued in a twelve-inch format contains sixteen ballads of unrequited love. *In the Wee Small Hours* provided a forum for Sinatra to express the anguish of a man still carrying a torch. Forty years after its commercial release, it remains great art.

The session of February 8, 1955, was done with a small group consisting of a piano, celeste, guitar, bass, and drums. It may be Sinatra at his intimate best. On ''Glad to Be Unhappy,'' Sinatra's wistful approach to Lorenz Hart's lyrics has a tenderness that evokes the essence of unfulfilled love. His friend and piano player for forty-five years, Bill Miller, paints a somber mood with his intricate playing in the framework of an exquisite Nelson Riddle arrangement.

Hart's lyric, often regarded as his personal credo on romantic love, was written for the Broadway musical *On Your Toes* in 1936. The song was introduced by Doris Carson and David Morris.

Sinatra's performances of the song would be confined to concerts in the mid- to late 1950s. He would sing the verse on *Francis Albert Sinatra Does His Thing*, a CBS-TV special on November 25, 1968, available on video and laser disc from Warner Bros.

38

''What Is This Thing Called Love?''

Words and music by Cole Porter
Recorded February 16, 1955, in Los Angeles
Arranged by Nelson Riddle
CD: *In the Wee Small Hours* (CDP 7-96826-2) and *Frank Sinatra—The Capitol Years* (C2-94777 CDP 7-94318-2)

A question straight from the heart—and a consummate performance by Sinatra. The master recording came on take 21.

This song evolved during the making of the record, not unusual for a Sinatra recording session. On the first take, the running time was almost four minutes and Riddle's arrangement was a bit too complex. The arrangement was simplified, the song was cut down to two minutes and thirty-five seconds, and mutes were put on the horns. The tempo was altered on different takes and Sinatra improvised on high and low notes throughout the session.

The song is Cole Porter's most popular composition—after "Begin the Beguine." It was written for the English musical theater production of *Wake Up and Dream* and introduced by Elsie Carlisle. The New York run opened on December 30, 1929, with Frances Shelley performing the song. The song became a hit for many artists, but none would perform it better than Sinatra.

An up-tempo version of the song was recorded for Sinatra's *Perfectly Frank* radio program in the winter of 1954. It is available only on an unauthorized CD.

39

''Mood Indigo''

Words and music by Edward Kennedy "Duke" Ellington, Irving Mills, and Albany "Barney" Bigard
Recorded February 16, 1955, in Los Angeles
Arranged by Nelson Riddle
CD: *In the Wee Small Hours* (CDP 7-96826-2)

A great reading by Sinatra of a great song—and a fabulous blues arrangement by Nelson Riddle. Both the vocal and the chart possess a seamless quality that gives a wonderful texture to the tune. Sinatra begins with the chorus, proceeds to the verse, and returns to the chorus. Duke Ellington adored it.

Under the gun, Ellington composed the tune in fifteen minutes, right before a recording date scheduled for October 30, 1930. The song was introduced as "Dreamy Blues." The following year, the song was retitled "Mood Indigo" and became a major hit. In 1974, it was among the eight original songs to receive a Grammy award as a historic recording.

Sinatra did not record much of Ellington—only four songs—the most obvious oversight being "Solitude," a song that seems ideally suited for the singer. In 1968, Sinatra teamed with Ellington for an album, *Francis A. and Edward K.*, an interesting work of eight songs, featuring long jazz charts by arranger Billy May.

---

*B*ill Miller, Sinatra's friend and piano player since 1951, shared with *Sinatra 101* his eight all-time favorite Sinatra recordings:

1. "Only the Lonely"
2. "I Get Along Without You Very Well"
3. "I Hadn't Anyone 'til You"
4. "Guess I'll Hang My Tears Out to Dry"
5. "I've Got You Under My Skin"
6. "The Lady Is a Tramp"
7. "Don'cha Go 'Way Mad"
8. "One for My Baby"

40

"I Get Along Without You Very Well"

Words by Jane Brown Thompson and music by Hoagy Carmichael
Recorded February 17, 1955, in Los Angeles
Arranged by Nelson Riddle
CD: *In the Wee Small Hours* (CDP 7-96826-2)

One of Sinatra's top five ballad recordings. Arranger Nelson Riddle added twelve violins to the session. The result is a weepy sound from the string section that accentuates Sinatra's strong emotional reading. A sadness in Sinatra's voice makes the song even more poignant.

The genesis of the song lies in an unsigned poem by Jane Brown Thompson. A university student gave a copy of the poem to Hoagy Carmichael. Before securing the rights to the poem, Carmichael composed the melody. It took Carmichael many years before he was able to locate the lyricist. On the eve of January 19, 1940—the day Dick Powell introduced the song on radio—Thompson died. Never a hit, the song was performed by Carmichael and Jane Russell in the 1952 movie *The Las Vegas Story*.

Sinatra performed the song in concert in the seventies and eighties to the Riddle arrangement. A memorable performance by Sinatra was recorded in London at the Royal

Festival Hall on November 16, 1970. It is included on a video and a laser disc available from Warner Bros.

41

''In the Wee Small Hours of the Morning''

Words by Bob Hilliard and music by David Mann
Recorded February 17, 1955, in Los Angeles
Arranged by Nelson Riddle
CD: *In the Wee Small Hours* (CDP 7-96826-2) and *Frank Sinatra—The Capitol Years* (C2-94777 CDP 7-94318-2)

Sinatra—the surrogate for our deepest wounds—in a definitive recording that wasn't meant to happen.

Bob Hilliard and David Mann had Nat King Cole in mind when they composed the tune. But the song ended up with Sinatra—to become the title track on the album that many consider to be Sinatra's finest work.

The desolate piano introduction by Bill Miller establishes a theme that Sinatra never abandons. As music critic Pete Welding noted: "Ava Gardner may have left scars, but as happens so often with great artists, personal pain translated into artistic achievement."

Sinatra recorded the song again on April 29, 1963, for Reprise, available on *Sinatra's Sinatra* (Rep. CD 1010-2) and on *A Man and His Music* (Rep. CD 1016-2). Both the Capitol and Reprise recordings were arranged by Nelson Riddle.

A song which was closely identified with him, Sinatra performed it a few times on television and with some regularity in concert.

42

"When Your Lover Has Gone"

Words and music by Einar A. Swan
Recorded February 17, 1955, in Los Angeles
Arranged by Nelson Riddle
CD: *In the Wee Small Hours* (CDP 7-96826-2)

The penultimate track from the legendary sessions of February 1955. Sinatra's contemplative interpretation and Riddle's beautifully crafted string arrangement combine to capture the overall theme of *Wee Small Hours*.

Here Sinatra unearths a lost treasure—Einar Swan's only successful composition. The lyric is particularly brilliant ("At daybreak, there is no sunrise, when your lover has gone. . . ."). Written in 1931 and introduced in the film *Blonde Crazy*, starring James Cagney, the song became only a minor commercial hit for Gene Austin.

Sinatra had recorded the song for Columbia on December 19, 1944. The track is available on *Frank Sinatra—The Columbia Years 1943–1952* (CXK-48673-CK-52867) and on *The Voice—The Columbia Years* (C4K-40343-CK-40634). He would perform the song throughout his career—on radio, television, and in concert.

*A*t a private party many years after the *Wee Small Hours* sessions, Sinatra, sitting on a stool, with just a piano for accompaniment, sang the songs from the album to a small audience that included a notable guest. Her name was Ava Gardner. She had been the catalyst for the album, and she would be an influence on the great torch songs to follow.

43

"Learnin' the Blues"

Words and music by Dolores Vicki Silvers
Recorded March 23, 1955, in Los Angeles
Arranged by Nelson Riddle
CD: *Frank Sinatra: The Capitol Collector's Series* (CDP 7-92160-2) and *Frank Sinatra—The Capitol Years* (C2-94777 CDP 7-94318-2)

A song written for Sinatra by a young woman from Philadelphia. It became Sinatra's biggest hit single at Capitol, and one of the great jukebox songs of all time.

Two hours and thirty-one takes in the making, "Learnin' the Blues" was the only song recorded at the session of March 23, 1955. From the onset, Sinatra had problems getting a handle on the arrangement by Riddle. Further complicating matters, he could not find a suitable approach to the lyric. After many takes, an undertone of anger worked

its way into his vocal. This comes through on the master—
the thirty-first take. The hard work paid off: For the next
fifteen years, the recording would be a mainstay in juke-
boxes throughout the Western world.

Sinatra recorded the song again on October 2, 1962, for
Reprise, backed by Count Basie and His Orchestra. The arrangement is by Neal Hefti. Sinatra sounds tired and his
voice is raspy, making for a disappointing track. The recording is available on *Sinatra–Basie* (Rep. CD 1008-2) and
on *A Man and His Music* (Rep. CD 1016-2).

Sinatra performed the song only a few times on TV and
for just a short time in concert. Despite its commercial success, it never became a Sinatra "must do" song. It was
taped for the award-winning TV special *A Man and His Music*, but was deleted from the broadcast that aired on November 24, 1965.

44

"I Thought About You"

Words by Johnny Mercer and music by James Van Heusen
Recorded January 9, 1956, in Los Angeles
Arranged by Nelson Riddle
CD: *Songs for Swingin' Lovers* (CDP 7-46570-2) and *Frank
    Sinatra—The Capitol Years* (C2-94777 CDP 7-94318-2)

Many critics consider *Swingin' Lovers* to be Sinatra's
greatest album. Without question, it is one of the most
influential. The art of popular singing and the urban ethos

of the time both fell under its power. You simply weren't singing if you weren't singing like Sinatra. Whitney Balliett, jazz critic for *The New Yorker*, referred to it as "the school of Sinatra singing." More than a few singers of the day fashioned careers by imitating the sound that Sinatra pioneered on *Swingin' Lovers*.

Sinatra's vocal on "I Thought About You" is incredibly smooth. At this point, Sinatra and Riddle were in full synch, and it was becoming harder to distinguish one from the other in terms of overall effect. Riddle employed a thirty-five-piece orchestra for the session. A big-band sound and Sinatra's skillful vocal created a delightful experience for the listener.

A pop tune written in 1939, the song was originally a hit for Benny Goodman and His Orchestra, with Mildred Bailey on vocal.

Sinatra first recorded the song at Capitol on June 30, 1955. The arrangement was dramatically different from the 1956 recording. It lacked the vitality and modernity of the *Swingin' Lovers* version. It is available on an unauthorized CD.

45

"You Make Me Feel So Young"

Words by Mack Gordon and music by Josef Myrow
Recorded January 9, 1956, in Los Angeles
Arranged by Nelson Riddle
CD: *Songs for Swingin' Lovers* (CDP 7-46570-2) and *Frank Sinatra—The Capitol Years* (C2-94777 CDP 7-94318-2)

A jubilant arrangement by Riddle, a joyous vocal by Sinatra, and a wonderful track. For decades to come, Sinatra would frequently open his concerts with this song.

Written in 1946 for the film musical *Three Little Girls in Blue*, the tune was introduced by Charles Smith and Vera-Ellen, whose voices were dubbed by Del Porter and Carol Stewart.

A concert performance from early 1966, in which Sinatra is backed by the Count Basie Orchestra against a driving Quincy Jones chart, is available on *Sinatra at the Sands* (Rep. CD 1019-2) and on *The Reprise Collection* (Rep. CD 9-26340-2). A second studio recording on July 6, 1993, appears on *Duets* (CDP 0777-7-89611-2). It is a credible performance by the seventy-seven-year-old Sinatra. A concert recording of the song from the Sands on November 5, 1961, remains unreleased.

46

``Memories of You''

Words by Andy Razaf and music by Eubie Blake
Recorded January 9, 1956, in Los Angeles
Arranged by Nelson Riddle
CD: *Frank Sinatra—The Capitol Years* (C2-94777 CDP 7-94318-2)

Possibly the most unjustly neglected recording Sinatra ever made. This track, from the *Swingin' Lovers* sessions of 1956, was not commercially released until 1973. Capitol already had one ballad on the *Swingin' Lovers* album—"We'll Be Together Again"—and apparently it was decided that one was enough. The irony is that the recording may be Nelson Riddle's finest ballad chart, and Sinatra's vocal range and control are impeccable.

Composed for the revue *Lew Leslie's Blackbirds of 1930*, the tune was introduced by Minto Cato. It was a hit for Glen Gray and the Casa Loma Orchestra and for Louis Armstrong. Later it became the theme song for Sonny Dunham and His Orchestra.

Sinatra made a second recording of the song for Capitol on September 11, 1961 in a fine arrangement by Axel Stordahl. The track appears on *Point of No Return* (CDP 7-48334-2).

47

"I've Got You Under My Skin"

Words and music by Cole Porter
Recorded January 12, 1956, in Los Angeles
Arranged by Nelson Riddle
CD: *Songs for Swingin' Lovers* (CDP 7-46570-2), *Frank Sinatra Sings the Select Cole Porter* (CDP 7-96611-2), and *Frank Sinatra—The Capitol Years* (C2-94777 CDP 7-94318-2)

The single greatest recording of Sinatra's career. The driving sound of the brass section, featuring trombonist Milt Bernhart, combined with Sinatra's rhythmic cadence, is a transcendent moment in the history of popular music. Sinatra, the perfectionist, was not satisfied until the twenty-second take. The sound that Sinatra and Riddle created on "Skin" would be often imitated but never quite equaled.

Cole Porter wrote the song for the 1936 Hollywood musical *Born to Dance*. It was sung in the film by Virginia Bruce. That same year, it was a hit for both Ray Noble and His Orchestra and for Hal Kemp and His Orchestra.

Sinatra and Riddle teamed up for another recording of the song at Reprise on April 30, 1963. A terrific track, it merely lacks the magic of the first recording. It is available on *Sinatra's Sinatra* (Rep. CD 1010-2) and on *A Man and His Music* (Rep. CD 1016-2). Live recordings are available on *Sinatra and Sextet: Live in Paris* (Rep. CD 9-45487-2), performed on June 5, 1962; on *Sinatra at the Sands* (Rep. CD 1019-2), performed January 26–February 1, 1966, also available on *The Reprise Collection* (Rep. CD 9-26340-2); and on *Frank Sinatra/The Main Event—Live* (Rep. CD 2207-2), recorded in Buffalo, New York, on October 4, 1974. Finally, there is a recording done for *Duets* (CDP 0777-7-89611-2) on July 1, 1993. The voice is deeper and rougher around the edges but, incredibly, the timbre of his voice at seventy-seven is strikingly similar to that on the 1963 Reprise recording.

Sinatra performed a rare ballad rendition of "Skin" at a tribute to Cole Porter at the University of Southern California on February 12, 1967. His sole accompaniment was pianist Roger Edens. The track is available on an unauthorized CD.

Following the rehearsal of "Skin" by the musicians, the usually imperturbable sidemen gave Nelson Riddle a standing ovation in appreciation of his great chart. Asked in 1984 if he had any idea at the time how monumental his work with Sinatra would become, Riddle replied, "Hell, no! It was a lot of hard work and there were deadlines to meet. I was just glad to get them done on time."

48

``Too Marvelous for Words''

Words by Johnny Mercer and music by Richard A. Whiting
Recorded January 16, 1956, in Los Angeles
Arranged by Nelson Riddle
CD: *Songs for Swingin' Lovers* (CDP 7-46570-2) and *Frank Sinatra—The Capitol Years* (C2-94777 CDP 7-94318-2)

The fourth of five recordings Sinatra would cut on January 16, 1956. A wonderful collaboration between singer and arranger, Sinatra lets the beat carry him from a moderate tempo to a rousing climactic note. The last swing chart done for the *Swingin' Lovers* album, ``Too Marvelous for Words'' is an exclamation point at the end of a monumental work.

The tune was introduced in the 1937 Warner Bros. musical *Ready, Willing and Able* in a big production number featuring Ross Alexander, Winifred Shaw, and a giant typewriter. That year, Bing Crosby took the song to number one with the Jimmy Dorsey Orchestra.

At the Olympia in Paris on June 5, 1962, Sinatra would deliver a drop-dead rendition of the song, available on *Sinatra and Sextet: Live in Paris* (Rep. CD 9-45487-2). He would perform the song on television and in concert throughout the fifties and sixties.

49

``Everything Happens to Me''

Words by Tom Adair and music by Matt Dennis
Recorded April 4, 1956, in Los Angeles
Arranged by Nelson Riddle
CD: *Close to You and More* (CDP 7 46572-2: out of print) and
  Frank Sinatra Concepts (CDP 0777-7-99956-2)

This introspective lament of shattered dreams receives a gentle reading by Sinatra, in spite of an angry subtext. He was at his vocal peak in 1956.

With brilliant charts set to chamber music, *Close to You* is the most intimate of Sinatra's work with Riddle—yet it is Sinatra's least successful concept album at Capitol Records in terms of commercial sales. The recordings were made in the spring and fall of 1956 with the Hollywood String Quartet, consisting of two violins, a cello, and a viola. The quartet was backed by a nine-piece orchestra for three sessions, with a seven-piece ensemble brought in for the final date.

A pop tune written in 1941, the song was first recorded by Tommy Dorsey and His Orchestra on February 7, 1941, with vocal by Frank Sinatra. A moderate hit for the band, the recording is available on *The Song Is You* (RCA 07863-66353-2).

Sinatra recorded the song again, on September 24, 1974, and on April 8, 1981, in both cases with different lyrics than those on the 1941 and 1956 recordings. The 1981 track is outstanding. It would rival the 1956 recording if the lyrics were of a higher order. Both songs are on *The Complete Sinatra* (Rep. CD 46013-2).

50

"With Every Breath I Take"

Words by Leo Robin and music by Ralph Rainger
Recorded April 5, 1956, in Los Angeles
Arranged by Nelson Riddle
CD: *Close To You and More* (CDP 7-46572-2: out of print) and
    Frank Sinatra Concepts (CDP 0777-7-99956-2)

The masterpiece from the *Close to You* album, with several attributes that make it extraordinary: Riddle's marvelously understated arrangement, Sinatra's masterful vocal control, and Sinatra's uncanny ability to read a heartfelt ballad. It is some of the finest vocal work he would ever do. There is an intimacy conveyed by Sinatra in this work that is rarely attained by any artist. Here he achieves a self-confessional tone that seems to bring him right into the room with the listener. The result is an achievement of powerful romantic intensity.

The song was first sung by Bing Crosby in the 1934 film musical *Here Is My Heart*. At the time, Crosby was at the peak of his popularity. For Crosby, it would be one of three bestselling songs from the movie.

In early 1950, Sinatra sang the song on the *Lite Up Time* radio program.

In 1956, Leonard Feather polled the top one hundred jazz musicians in the world for their all-time favorite vocalists and instrumentalists. Sinatra was named by his contemporaries as the greatest male vocalist—by a three to one margin over Nat King Cole.

51

"I Wish I Were in Love Again"

Words by Lorenz Hart and music by Richard Rodgers
Recorded November 20, 1956, in Los Angeles
Arranged by Nelson Riddle
CD: *A Swingin' Affair!* (CDP 7-94518-2) and *Frank Sinatra— The Capitol Years* (C2-94777 CDP 7-94319-2)

A recording that stands out for two distinct reasons: the chemistry created when Lorenz Hart's romantic cynicism mixes with Sinatra's urban cool, and a driving tempo from Riddle that enables the singer to joyfully convey the satire and resignation that characterize the song. Sinatra's innate rhythmic ability is beautifully spotlighted on this chart. His syncopated, inflected reading of Hart's lyrics is brilliant. The "jazz singer" shines through on this particular recording.

The song is a tongue-in-cheek romp about the state of being in love, featuring brilliant and entertaining lines from Hart, such as "the self-deception that believes the lies" and "the conversations with flying plates."

Introduced by Grace McDonald and Rolly Pickert in the 1937 Broadway musical *Babes in Arms*, the song was later performed by Judy Garland and Mickey Rooney in the film *Words and Music* in 1948.

A performance of the song was masterfully done by Sinatra on his TV show on November 22, 1957.

52

"The Lady Is a Tramp"

Words by Lorenz Hart and music by Richard Rodgers
Recorded November 26, 1956, in Los Angeles
Arranged by Nelson Riddle
CD: *A Swingin' Affair!* (CDP 7-94518-2) and *Frank Sinatra Sings the Select Rodgers and Hart* (CDP 0777-7-80323-2)

Second only to "Skin" as Sinatra's greatest swing recording. Bill Miller's piano intro sets the pace for an energetic tour de force by the singer. The interpolations in the lyrics that Sinatra would introduce throughout the years are legendary. Probably no serious Sinatraphile remembers what the original lyrics actually are. There is an alternate take available on *Frank Sinatra—The Capitol Years* (C2-94777 CDP 94319-2).

Written by Rodgers and Hart for the 1937 Broadway musical *Babes in Arms,* the song was originally sung by Mitzi Green. Sinatra performed the song in the film version of *Pal Joey* in 1957.

Sinatra liked to refer to this song as a "gasser." An outstanding concert performance is available on *Sinatra and Sextet: Live in Paris* (Rep. CD 9-45487-2), from June 5, 1962. A second live version is available on *Frank Sinatra/ The Main Event —Live* (Rep. CD 2207-2), from October 13, 1974, with a Billy Byers arrangement. On July 1, 1993, Sinatra recorded the song for *Duets* (CDP 0777-7-89611-2) using the Byers chart.

What may be the definitive recording of "Tramp" is not available on a commercial CD. Sinatra's recording of the song on May 23, 1957—on the Columbia sound stage for *Pal Joey*—came after Sinatra had been polishing his interpretation of the song in concert for eight months. He simply nails it. The track is available on the Columbia film video and on a laser disc.

53

``From This Moment On''

Words and music by Cole Porter
Recorded November 28, 1956, in Los Angeles
Arranged by Nelson Riddle
CD: *A Swingin' Affair!* (CDP 7-94518-2) and *Frank Sinatra Sings the Select Cole Porter* (CDP 7-96611-2)

The final session for the great concept albums of 1956, a pinnacle year for Sinatra in which he would record forty-seven songs for concept albums and establish himself as the premier vocalist of the day. This marvelous recording begins at a leisurely pace, building to a crescendo of horns that seems to propel the vocal. Sinatra had proven to the world that he could swing, and the singer and his arranger had breathed new life into a number of Cole Porter compositions with imaginative up-tempo interpretations.

Composed for the Broadway play *Out of This World* in 1950, the song had been dropped from the show before opening night. William Eythe and Priscilla Gillette had introduced the song in out-of-town tryouts. Eventually it surpassed the popularity of the songs that made the final cut, and it was featured in an elaborate production number in the film version of *Kiss Me Kate* in 1953. Ann Miller and Tommy Rall performed the song.

Sinatra performed the song in concert and on TV in the mid- to late 1950s.

54

"Lonely Town"

Words by Betty Comden and Adolph Green, music by Leonard Bernstein
Recorded April 29, 1957, in Los Angeles
Arranged by Gordon Jenkins
CD: *Where Are You?* (CDP 7-91209-2)

Sinatra liked the sound of strings in a ballad. He felt it added class and a dramatic content to the recording. For his first four years at Capitol he had worked almost exclusively with arranger Nelson Riddle. Now enter Gordon Jenkins. His arrangements for Sinatra would be less subtle than Riddle's. Wrought with detail and intensity, they would evoke a darker side of the Sinatra persona. With Jenkins, Sinatra would produce some of his finest work.

"Lonely Town" is a cry from the heart of the urbanite, alone. The isolation is richly portrayed in Sinatra's haunting vocal. There is more of an element of despair in his singing than ever before.

Sinatra had been greatly concerned about the natural wear and tear that time had exacted on his vocal cords. As he was listening to the final playback of "Lonely Town," Sinatra turned to a friend and declared: "Gordon Jenkins has saved my life."

A 1944 composition for the Broadway musical *On the*

Town, the song was introduced on stage by John Battles. The song was omitted from the 1949 film adaptation starring Gene Kelly and Frank Sinatra. The latter was not pleased by the producer's decision.

Sinatra performed the song in concert through the remainder of the decade and into the 1970s and 1980s.

When asked by *Sinatra 101* to name his all-time favorite Sinatra recordings, Jonathan Schwartz, host of the weekly *Sinatra Saturday* show on WQEW radio in New York, cited five albums plus thirty-six single recordings with little hesitation. Following is his train of thought, basically verbatim:

Every recording on the albums *In the Wee Small Hours* and *Songs for Swingin' Lovers* (that's thirty-one songs); *Swingin' Affair* (except the track "No One Ever Tells You"); *Frank Sinatra Sings for Only the Lonely*; and *Francis Albert Sinatra and Antonio Carlos Jobim*.

"I Have Dreamed"; "It's Sunday"; "Moonlight Serenade"; "The Coffee Song" (second version); "Don't Like Goodbyes"; "Love Locked Out"; "April in Paris" (Capitol version); "All of Me"; "Just One of Those Things"; "Like Someone in Love"; "Where Are You?"; "Lonely Town"; "My Blue Heaven" (Capitol version); "None But the Lonely Heart" (Capitol version); "A Cottage for Sale"; "Here's That Rainy Day"; "River Stay Away from My Door"; "Day In, Day Out" (second Capitol ballad version with Nelson Riddle); "My Shining Hour"; "New York, New York"; "Hey Look, No Crying"; "Someone to Light Up My

Life" (second Jobim album); "Everything Happens to Me" (1981 version); "Just as Though You Were Here" (Reprise version); "The Nearness of You" (Columbia version); "How Deep Is the Ocean?" (Columbia version); "The Last Dance" (Billy May arrangement); "The Birth of the Blues"; "I've Got a Crush on You" (Columbia version); "It Never Entered My Mind" (Columbia version); "Night and Day" (Columbia version); "East of the Sun" (Reprise version); "Come Rain or Come Shine" (Don Costa arrangement); "Send in the Clowns" (second recording); "Dream Away"; "Wandering."

55

"Witchcraft"

Words by Carolyn Leigh and music by Cy Coleman
Recorded May 20, 1957, in Los Angeles
Arranged by Nelson Riddle
CD: *Frank Sinatra: The Capitol Collector's Series* (CDP 7-92160-2) and *Frank Sinatra—The Capitol Years* (C2-94777 CDP 7-94319-2)

A very sexy turn by Mr. Sinatra. An insinuating vocal backed by a strong Nelson Riddle arrangement, the recording became a big hit in 1958. Riddle's arrangement would receive a Grammy nomination, and the song would remain closely linked with Sinatra throughout his career.

The tune was composed in 1957 and introduced by Gerry Matthews in Julius Monk's nightclub revue *Take Five*.

Sinatra recorded the song again on April 30, 1963, at Reprise, available on *Sinatra's Sinatra* (Rep. CD 1010-2) and on *A Man and His Music* (Rep. CD 1016-2). A third recording was done on July 9, 1993, for Capitol's *Duets* (CDP 0777-7-89611-2). In the Reprise vault is an unreleased concert recording from the Sands on November 5, 1961.

One of Sinatra's all-time perennials, he was still singing "Witchcraft" in concert in the mid-1990s.

The lyricist Carolyn Leigh wrote two of Sinatra's biggest hits in the 1950s. "Young at Heart" was Sinatra's first major hit at Capitol in 1954, and his first chart buster in eight years. "Witchcraft" was the follow-up hit to "All the Way" in January of 1958. Actually, it had been recorded four months before "All the Way," but Capitol delayed its release.

56

``Bewitched''

Words by Lorenz Hart and music by Richard Rodgers
Recorded August 13, 1957, in Los Angeles
Arranged by Nelson Riddle
CD: *Frank Sinatra Sings the Select Rodgers and Hart* (CDP 0777-
   7-80323-2) and the soundtrack from *Pal Joey* (CDP 7-
   91249-2: out of print)

A rich and warm reading by Sinatra, including a marvelous treatment of the verse. Nelson Riddle's orchestral arrangement superbly backs Sinatra on the chorus. Another Rodgers and Hart song and another remarkable interpretation by Sinatra and Riddle.

The song was introduced by Vivienne Segal in the 1940 Broadway hit *Pal Joey*. In the film version, Sinatra sang the tune. With its charming melody and sophisticated lyrics, the song became one of the all-time popular compositions from Rodgers and Hart.

For some unknown reason, Sinatra sang only a brief segment of the song in the film *Pal Joey*. The work sheets from Columbia Pictures do not show a complete take of the tune. The short version for the film was laid down three weeks prior to the Capitol recording.

A recording that resembled a full concert recital was done for Reprise on February 20, 1963, with a seventy-three-piece orchestra. The chart was written by Riddle. It appears on *The Concert Sinatra* (Rep. CD 1009-2). Sinatra recorded the song in 1994 for *Duets II* (CDP 7243-8-28103-2) to an arrangement by Patrick Williams. The vocal is a composite of live recordings taped in April. Orchestral tracks were laid down on May 17 and 18 at the Clinton Studio in New York.

---

*P*robably no one has done more to perpetuate the Rodgers and Hart legacy than Frank Sinatra. The singer's recordings of "I Wish I Were in Love Again," "The Lady Is a Tramp," "Bewitched" and many others constitute a passionate dictionary of romantic predicaments. The chemistry between the singer and the lyricist has everything to do with a sense of inner frailty and a trust in that frailty as an artistic resource.

STEPHEN HOLDEN,
The New York Times,
April 30, 1995

57

"All the Way"

Words by Sammy Cahn and music by James Van Heusen
Recorded August 13, 1957, in Los Angeles
Arranged by Nelson Riddle
CD. *Frank Sinatra: The Collector's Series* (CDP 7-92160-2)
  and *Frank Sinatra—The Capitol Years* (C2-94777 CDP
  7-94319-2)

Arguably the best hit single from Sinatra, and a power-house performance that would leave an indelible mark on his work at Capitol. Written at Sinatra's behest for his starring role as Joe E. Lewis in *The Joker Is Wild*, the song was an immediate sensation and winner of the 1957 Academy Award for best song.

Sinatra's 1957 Capitol recording was a smash hit, riding the music charts for thirty weeks. Its lyric was more profound than other Top 40 singles of the day. Riddle's arrangement is clean, augmenting but never competing with the vocal, and featuring a beautifully restrained string accompaniment. The film recording was cut on October 3, 1956, to a modified chart composed by Riddle.

Sinatra recorded the song for Reprise on April 29, 1963, to a Riddle arrangement. It appears on *Sinatra's Sinatra* (Rep. CD 1010-2) and on *A Man and His Music* (Rep. CD 1016-2). A concert recording, from the Olympia in Paris on June 5, 1962, remains unissued.

The song became a Sinatra standard, a number he would consistently perform for the rest of his career.

58

``April in Paris''

Words by Yip Harburg and music by Vernon Duke
Recorded October 3, 1957, in Los Angeles
Arranged by Billy May
CD: *Come Fly with Me* (CDP 7-48469-2)

The driving arrangements of Billy May brought a fresh if not irreverent style to Sinatra's swing tunes. He was the last of the three great arrangers at Capitol that played an integral role in the singer's recording career.

"April in Paris" was not Sinatra's favorite recording, but he considered it his *best* recording. Showing his versatility, May charted a gorgeous string arrangement that challenged Sinatra at his physical peak. The result is a windfall for the listener, as Sinatra meets the tough demands of May's extended passages. He hits incredibly lofty notes.

Composed in 1932 for the musical revue *Walk a Little Faster*, the song received its first reading from Evelyn Hoey. The first recording was done by Marian Chase for Liberty Records.

Sinatra had previously recorded the song to a tender arrangement by Axel Stordahl at Columbia Records on October 9, 1950. The recording appears on *Frank Sinatra— The Columbia Years 1943–1952* (CXK-48673-CK-52876) and on *The Voice—The Columbia Years* (C4K-40343-CK-40632). An excellent live track from June 5, 1962, is available on *Sinatra and Sextet: Live in Paris* (Rep. CD 9-45487-2) using a modified treatment of the original May chart. A concert track from the Sands in Las Vegas, recorded on November 5, 1961, remains in the Reprise vault.

Sinatra performed "April in Paris" for more than forty years. He seldom cheated the audience: he always sang it big.

---

*T*he great Billy May was hard pressed to name his all-time favorite Sinatra recordings for *Sinatra 101*. "There are many lovely and great arrangements by Nelson (Riddle), Gordon Jenkins, and Don Costa," said May. "This makes it a hard choice for arrangers."

May chose "Around the World in Eighty Days," "Come Fly with Me," and "Luck Be a Lady" as his favorite Sinatra single recordings. He picked *Sinatra Swings* from 1961 and *Trilogy: Past* from 1979 as his favorite Sinatra albums. Interestingly May referred to the 1961 Reprise album as both *Swing Along with Me* and *Sinatra Swings*. Capitol Records had contested the album title, *Swing Along with Me*, claiming it was too similar to its own Sinatra album, *Come Swing with Me!* Reprise subsequently retitled the album, *Sinatra Swings*. See page 120 for more details.

59

``Moonlight in Vermont''

Words by John Blackburn and music by Karl Suessdorf
Recorded October 3, 1957, in Los Angeles
Arranged by Billy May
CD: *Come Fly with Me* (CDP 7-48469-2)

May and Sinatra create a timeless work of art with a brilliant interpretation of a sublime ballad. The arranger builds a chart that magnifies the lyrical imagery of the song, and the singer responds with a definitive reading. One can almost see falling leaves, telegraph cables singing down the highway, ski trails on a mountainside, and moonlight in Vermont.

Written in 1944, the song was first recorded by Billy Butterfield and His Orchestra with vocal by Margaret Whiting. It was a moderate hit for Whiting in 1945 and again in 1954.

A terrific concert recording from June 5, 1962, is available on *Sinatra and Sextet: Live in Paris* (Rep. CD 9-45487-2). A live recording from April 1994 was combined with an orchestral track laid down on May 17, 1994, available on *Duets II* (CDP 7243-8-28103-2). A live track from the Sands, recorded by Reprise on November 5, 1961, remains unissued. Sinatra recorded the song again on October 14, 1994. It has not been released.

The Capitol recording session for "Moonlight in Vermont" makes for a wonderful listening experience. Sinatra does twelve takes. The singer comes across as very self-assured and in excellent form. The interesting repartee between singer and arranger throughout the session demonstrates the marvelous rapport that existed between Sinatra and Billy May.

60

"Angel Eyes"

Words by Earl Brent and music by Matt Dennis
Recorded May 29, 1958, in Los Angeles
Arranged by Nelson Riddle
CD: *Frank Sinatra Sings for Only the Lonely* (CDP 7-48471-2)
   and *Frank Sinatra—The Capitol Years* (C2-94777 CDP 7-94319-2)

A torch song from the album Sinatra considered to be his best work *Frank Sinatra Sings for Only the Lonely*. On an album of saloon songs, "Angel Eyes" is a quintessential saloon song. It is a classic tale of the classic loser: a guy in a bar at quarter to three in the morning, drowning his sorrows with drink, after his love has left him. The laughs and the drinks are on him, but there is no joy as he burdens the bartender with his miserable story. Sinatra is no stranger to the feeling, nor to the scenario, and on this recording he touches the very depths of despair.

Written for the 1953 film *Jennifer*, starring Ida Lupino and Howard Duff, the song was introduced on the silver screen by its composer, Matt Dennis. A song with great jazz attributes, it has been covered by many recording artists.

There is a live performance of "Angel Eyes" on *Sinatra at The Sands* (Rep. CD 1019-2), taped January 26 to February 1, 1966. A concert performance from October 4, 1974, in Buffalo, New York, appears on *Frank Sinatra/The Main Event—Live* (Rep. CD 2207-2). Two Capitol studio tracks remain unissued: a recording on May 5, 1958, and a recording on October 14, 1993, for the *Duets* project.

A t his "retirement" concert in June 1971, Sinatra closed the show with "Angel Eyes." In a cloud of cigarette smoke, Sinatra sang the final line: "Excuse me, while I disappear." The lights went out. When they came back up, he was gone. Tommy Thompson, writing for *Life* magazine, described it as "the single most stunning moment I have ever witnessed on a stage."

61

"Guess I'll Hang My Tears Out to Dry"

Words by Sammy Cahn and music by Jule Styne
Recorded May 29, 1958, in Los Angeles
Arranged by Nelson Riddle
CD: *Frank Sinatra Sings for Only the Lonely* (CDP 7-48471-2)
and *Frank Sinatra—The Capitol Years* (C2-94777 CDP-94320-2)

A Sinatra recording session had become theater. The lead actor and his supporting cast performed for an elite group of invited guests. Sinatra enacted three- and four-minute soliloquies not unlike Shakespearean dramas. He was combining great musical intellect with raw emotion. The stage was a recording studio and the actor/singer was working his way inside each song to illuminate every moment of it. Translated onto disc, the results were startling. A song of joy jumped out of the speakers and a hymn to despair touched the listener. Recording artistry had moved to a higher plane. A Sinatra album had become a major event. The question was how long Sinatra could continue to top himself.

"Guess I'll Hang My Tears Out to Dry" is a magnificent recording by Sinatra. Nelson Riddle composed an elaborate musical chart beginning with a complex guitar solo by Al Viola that set the stage for Sinatra's exquisite reading of the verse. The end product is a torch song of the highest order.

The tune was introduced in the 1944 Broadway musical *Glad to See You*. The play was a flop but the song survived to become one of the best collaborative songwriting efforts in the Cahn/Styne partnership. In 1945, Harry James and His Orchestra and Dinah Shore each recorded the song.

Sinatra's initial recording of the song was done at Columbia Records on July 30, 1946. Backed by an arrangement from "the mighty Stordahl," Sinatra gives it a lovely treatment. The track is available on *Frank Sinatra—The Columbia Years 1943–1952* (CXK-48673-CK-52869) and on *The Voice—The Columbia Years* (C4K-40343-CK-40634).

There is an unreleased recording from May 5, 1958, at Capitol. Sinatra had not been pleased with its orchestral work. Instead, he insisted that Al Viola accompany him on guitar for the recording. Sinatra recorded the song again for Capitol on July 9, 1993, for *Duets* (CDP 0777-7-89611-2) with Carly Simon's reading of "In the Wee Small Hours of the Morning" added to the final mix.

62

"Only the Lonely"

Words by Sammy Cahn and music by James Van Heusen
Recorded May 29, 1958, in Los Angeles
Arranged by Nelson Riddle
CD: *Frank Sinatra Sings for Only the Lonely* (CDP 7-48471-2)
   and *Frank Sinatra—The Capitol Years* (C2-94777 CDP 7-
   94320-2)

Pathos finds a voice. The title track from the album Sinatra considered to be his best work was done in nine takes. The emotional mood that Sinatra sustains throughout the album is compelling and definitive. The singer transforms melancholy and despair into great art. Was Sinatra invented for the ballad, or was the ballad invented for him?

Here there is an eerie detachment in Sinatra's vocal, a dissociation amplified by a haunting Riddle chart. The theme is intensely somber and the narrator issues a warning: Don't take love for granted, cling to each moment, and never let love go. A hymn to solitude in the wake of love lost, the song is a logical opening track for this concept album of personal pain.

The song was composed by Cahn and Van Heusen, who had also written the title track for "Come Fly with Me" and who would contribute four more title tracks to Sinatra concept albums.

There is no record that Sinatra ever performed the song in concert.

"*L*ush Life," the Billy Strayhorn classic written in 1938, was attempted by Sinatra at the May 29, 1958, session, but to no avail. There is a false start and then two incomplete takes. After the third take is aborted, Sinatra is caught on tape, venting his frustration: "It's not only tough enough with the way it is, but he's got some 'clydes' in there." One can only speculate that if Nelson Riddle had been present—he was touring with Nat King Cole—things might have turned out differently. Certainly a missed opportunity.

63

"Blues in the Night"

Words by Johnny Mercer and music by Harold Arlen
Recorded June 24, 1958, in Los Angeles
Arranged by Nelson Riddle
CD: *Frank Sinatra Sings for Only the Lonely* (CDP 7-48471-2)
   and *Frank Sinatra Sings the Select Johnny Mercer* (CDP 0777-7-80326-2)

Sinatra gets down and dirty and sings the blues in a strong, dramatic reading of Johnny Mercer's jazz-infused lyrics that are spiced with a residue of anger. The Arlen melody is brilliantly orchestrated by Nelson Riddle. A forty-five-piece orchestra was used for the session, but it does not dilute the intimate saloon atmosphere that Sinatra pursues and pulls off.

The song was the title track for the 1941 film *Blues in the Night*. The film tells the tale of a group of jazz musicians playing one-night stands. William Gillespie's was the first of many versions of the song featured in the film. The tune became a hit and a classic. Woody Herman and His Orchestra took it to number one in 1942. That same year, Jimmie Lunceford and His Orchestra and Dinah Shore each enjoyed hits with it.

Sinatra sang the song with the Tommy Dorsey band. There is no studio recording, but a radio air check from January 1942 appears on an unauthorized CD. The song would be performed by Sinatra in concert, most recently in the early 1980s.

---

*T*he whistling on ''Blues in the Night'' was done by . . . Sinatra. Nelson Riddle revealed this tidbit to Jonathan Schwartz on WNEW radio on September 12, 1982.

64

"One for My Baby"

Words by Johnny Mercer and music by Harold Arlen
Recorded June 26, 1958, in Los Angeles
Arranged by Nelson Riddle
CD: *Frank Sinatra Sings for Only the Lonely* (CDP 7-48471-2)
  and *Frank Sinatra Sings the Select Johnny Mercer* (CDP 0777-
  7-80326-2)

The master storyteller finds his magnum opus. What may be the greatest saloon song ever written may also be Sinatra's finest ballad work. The final recording made for the *Only the Lonely* project is a great moment in the Sinatra/Riddle collaboration.

The arrangement on the track is Riddle at his best. From the opening piano notes, it functions as a signature Sinatra sound. Through the years, Sinatra had carefully crafted the tune into the ultimate torch song. He had been refining it since the early fifties in his nightclub act. Bill Miller's piano had been the lone accompaniment. On August 11, 1954, Sinatra recorded the song at Warner Bros. for the film *Young at Heart*. This version was a precursor of the Capitol chart, featuring the same Miller piano accompaniment. The track has never been commercially released.

The song dates from the 1943 Fred Astaire film *The Sky's the Limit*. Astaire sang it in a mid-tempo waltzlike arrangement. Sinatra's Columbia recording of the song on August

11, 1947, is interpreted in a similar vein. It is included on *Frank Sinatra—The Columbia Years 1943–1952* (CXK-48673-CK-52871) and on *The Voice—The Columbia Years* (C4K-40343-CK-40634).

A superb concert recording from Sinatra appears on *Sinatra and Sextet: Live in Paris* (Rep. CD 9-45487-2), from June 5, 1962. A lesser version from the Sands performance of January 26 to February 1, 1966 is available on *Sinatra at the Sands* (Rep. CD 1019-2). A demo recording from June 24, 1958, was issued by Capitol on *Frank Sinatra—The Capitol Years* (C2-94777 CDP 7-94320-2). The most recent recording, for Capitol's *Duets* (CDP 0777-7-89611-2), was the final recording of the July 1, 1993, session. Completed in one take, with the Riddle arrangement from 1958, it is a symbiosis of great artistry and mortality. Here a very old man is recalling the passions of long ago and far away, in what could be the most moving and mournful of all recordings by Sinatra.

---

*I*n Palm Springs, California, on June 27, 1976, Sinatra performed a benefit concert. The venue was a large gymnasium without air-conditioning. The temperature hovered around 114 degrees. Sinatra sang with a small combo. He told the audience that a friend, Johnny Mercer, had passed away the previous day, and that he wanted to dedicate the next song to him. (Mercer actually died on June 25.) As Sinatra started to sing "One for My Baby," a hush fell over the crowd and a moment of pure magic took over the room. It was a stunning performance—as the self-proclaimed saloon singer paid his last respects to the man who had written the ultimate saloon song.

65

"Where or When"

Words by Lorenz Hart and music by Richard Rodgers
Recorded September 11, 1958, in Los Angeles
Arranged by Nelson Riddle
CD: *Frank Sinatra Sings for Only the Lonely* (CDP 7-48471-2)
   and *Frank Sinatra Sings the Select Rodgers and Hart* (CDP 0777-7-80323-2)

The finest recording ever made of "Where or When" sat in the Capitol vault for more than fifteen years. The mystery was solved only recently. In September 1958, Sinatra was looking for a saloon song to sing in the clubs. At the recording session for the song, a piano solo by Bill Miller accompanies Sinatra until one minute and forty-three seconds into the track, when a thirty-two-piece orchestra joins him at the bridge and propels the song for forty-one seconds to an astonishing climactic note by the singer. Unfortunately, before the master recording, which would come on take seven, Sinatra had soured on the concept. He is caught on tape saying, "It doesn't sound like a saloon." Not until the 1980s would the recording appear on compact disc, when Capitol added it to the CD release of *Only the Lonely*.

The tune was composed for the 1937 Broadway musical *Babes in Arms,* sung by Mitzi Green and Ray Heatherton. Recorded that same year by Hal Kemp and His Orchestra, it became the biggest hit in the nation.

An early ballad version by Sinatra was recorded at Columbia Records on January 29, 1945, to a Stordahl arrangement and with the choral support of the Ken Lane Singers. It appears on *Frank Sinatra—The Columbia Years 1943–1952* (CXK-48673-CK-52867) and on *The Voice—The Columbia Years* (C4K-40343-CK-40632). In the mid-1960s, Sinatra turned to a swinging arrangement by Billy Byers. A concert version was recorded during the Sands engagement of January 26 to February 1, 1966, available on *Sinatra at the Sands* (Rep. CD 1019-2). It is the definitive up-tempo rendition of the song. A studio recording of the Byers arrangement was done on October 14, 1993, for *Duets II* (CDP 7243 8-28103-2). An unreleased recording from the *Duets* project was taped on July 1, 1993.

Sinatra performed the song throughout his career.

---

*A*t the September 11, 1958, session, Sinatra was scheduled to record a song written by Ben Allen and Sinatra's manager, Hank Sanicola. The tune had been scheduled several times for recording, but never done. After the final take for "Where or When," Sinatra was asked again if he wanted to take a crack at "Who's in Your Arms Tonight?" Sinatra was frank: "It's over! Forget it! We'll do it at another date. This may go on for four years. We'll keep bringing it in all the time, and you'll keep trying to get me to do it." He never did.

66

"Something's Gotta Give"

Words and music by Johnny Mercer
Recorded December 9, 1958, in Los Angeles
Arranged by Billy May
CD: *Come Dance with Me* (CDP 7-48468-2) and *Frank Sinatra Sings the Select Johnny Mercer* (CDP 0777-7-80326-2)

Sinatra at his uninhibited best. Ripping through a driving Billy May chart, he ends the recording with a wonderfully hip aside to the band. He is on a roll.

In fact, he is on the greatest roll of his life, which started in 1953. The album *Come Dance with Me* is another career highlight. Neatly packaged in fabulous Basie-like charts from May, it would remain on the *Billboard* album chart for 140 weeks, a personal best for Sinatra. In 1959, the disc would win Grammy awards for best male vocal performance, best arrangements, and album of the year.

The song was introduced by Fred Astaire in the 1955 film musical *Daddy Long Legs*. Johnny Mercer, famous for his lyrics, once claimed he wasn't very good at writing a melody. This song disproves the self-effacement.

"Something's Gotta Give" was seldom performed by Sinatra. He joined the McGuire Sisters in an engaging rendition of the song on his television show on November 15, 1957. There are no known concert performances.

---

*J*n an interview in 1991, Billy May reflected on the tribulations that made the *Come Dance with Me* sessions particularly trying: "It was a miracle we got it done. Frank and I were so involved with other projects at the time. I was all over the place with TV, movies, and other records. Frank was even busier. He was doing movie after movie, playing nightclubs, [appearing on] TV, and moving into producing. We were very lucky. Everybody was ready and Frank was such a pro. We didn't have an extra day—front or back. I must say I was very pleased with the results. A hell of an album."

67

"Here's That Rainy Day"

Words by Johnny Burke and music by James Van Heusen
Recorded March 25, 1959, in Los Angeles
Arranged by Gordon Jenkins
CD: *No One Cares* (CDP 7-94519-2) and *Frank Sinatra—The Capitol Years* (C2-94777 CDP 7-94320-2)

A dark ballad that takes full advantage of the fact that, by the late 1950s, Sinatra's voice had dropped a shade or two.

The evolution enabled Sinatra to bring greater dimension to ballads. He was straining now for the high notes, which conveyed to the listener a greater sense of pain and fed the themes of anguish, heartbreak, and loneliness that were at the core of the ballads he chose to perform. As the years passed and the high notes moved even further away, Sinatra would use it to his advantage, effectively creating vocal interpretations with greater insight. In "Here's That Rainy Day," Johnny Burke's metaphor for the end of a love affair provides a vehicle for the combined skills of Sinatra and arranger Gordon Jenkins, as Jenkins constructs an ominous setting for Sinatra's poignant vocal.

Burke and James Van Heusen wrote the song for the Broadway musical *Carnival in Flanders* in 1953. The tune was performed in the play by John Raitt. The show was a failure but the song went on to become a cabaret classic.

In the Reprise vault are two unissued concert recordings of the song by Sinatra: at the Sands on November 5, 1961, and as part of a "saloon trilogy" from Carnegie Hall on April 8, 1974. Sinatra would define and redefine this tune for almost three decades—but there was never any doubt who "owned" the song.

Sinatra, who in concert rarely deviated from his planned program, made an exception on August 25, 1975, at the Performing Arts Center in Saratoga, New York. Nearing the end of the show, he spotted in the audience his old friend Chester—the composer James Van Heusen. "Chester, I didn't know you were here," announced Sinatra. "Why didn't somebody tell me?"

Sinatra walked over to the piano for a brief conference with Bill Miller, then made his way to the lip of the stage, leaning over to Van Heusen: "This is for you, Chester." Sinatra then treated the audience to a touching rendition of "Here's That Rainy Day."

68

"A Cottage for Sale"

Words by Willard Robison and music by Larry Conley
Recorded March 26, 1959, in Los Angeles
Arranged by Gordon Jenkins
CD: *No One Cares* (CDP 7 94519-2)

Who but Sinatra could bring the maximum interpretation to a lament of such excruciating heartbreak? A somber, restrained arrangement by Gordon Jenkins allows Sinatra the forum to find the darkest recesses in a song of loss, despair, and interminable sadness. It may be the darkest of all Sinatra songs for losers. It may be the darkest of all songs on the subject of divorce.

The song was composed in 1930, introduced by Willard Robison and His Deep River Orchestra. A tune that was popular during the early years of the Great Depression, it was a hit single for Guy Lombardo and His Royal Canadians. A strong melodic line has allowed other artists to reinvent the song as a swinging jazz number.

The Capitol recording appears to be Sinatra's only performance of the song.

No One Cares is Sinatra's most somber work. He often referred to it as the suicide album. A funereal quality is created by the singer and the arranger. It is as if love and light and hope have all been extinguished. It is unrequited love taken to the limit.

---

*I*n nine years at Capitol Records, Sinatra recorded a total of 330 tracks.

69

"It's All Right with Me"

Words and music by Cole Porter
Recorded August 27, 1959, in Los Angeles
Arranged by Nelson Riddle
CD: *Can-Can Soundtrack* (CDP 7-91248-2: out of print) and
Frank Sinatra Sings the Select Cole Porter (CDP 7-96611-2)

Probably the most intimate singing Sinatra has ever done, the song was recorded on the sound stage at Twentieth Century-Fox during the making of *Can-Can*. Sinatra is right on the mike. This is difficult for a singer to do, but Sinatra's impeccable diction allows him the latitude to accomplish it with room to spare. A Parisian-flavored arrangement by

Nelson Riddle sets the mood as Sinatra gives a tender romantic reading. The recording is a marvelous display of Sinatra's ability for interpretation and a testament to his incredible vocal control.

Cole Porter composed the song for the Broadway musical *Can-Can*, completing it in March 1953 as the play was about to open for its out-of-town run at the Shubert Theater in Philadelphia. The tune was introduced by Peter Cookson. Sinatra performed the song in the 1960 film version. The slow tempo was done at the suggestion of Cole Porter.

Sinatra recorded the song again on April 16, 1984, in New York to a swinging Sam Nestico arrangement. It is available on *L.A. Is My Lady* from Qwest (CD-WPCP-3604), issued in Japan; and on a CD issued in Brazil (CD 925145-2). It is also available on *The Complete Sinatra* from Reprise (Rep. CD 46013-2).

---

*T*hroughout the 1950s, Columbia issued Sinatra albums comprised of single recordings from his years at Columbia. These albums were in contrast to the great conceptual albums Sinatra was creating for Capitol. *Nice 'n' Easy* was Capitol's revenge. With the exception of the title track, the songs on the album are all remakes of Sinatra's earlier Columbia recordings. With beautiful arrangements by Nelson Riddle, Sinatra recorded and released his most romantic album for Capitol Records. *Nice 'n' Easy* would top the *Billboard* album chart and remain a bestseller for eighty-six weeks.

70

``The Nearness of You''

Words by Ned Washington and music by Hoagy Carmichael
Recorded March 2, 1960, in Los Angeles
Arranged by Nelson Riddle
CD: *Nice 'n' Easy* (CDP 7-96827-2)

Sinatra at his romantic best. A lush romantic chart by Nelson Riddle and marvelous piano work by Bill Miller heighten the effect of Sinatra's imposing vocal. The track sounds as fresh today as then, more than thirty-six years ago.

"The Nearness of You" was the original title track for what was to become the *Nice 'n' Easy* album. It was deleted from the album after the new title track was recorded. Two years later, it showed up on the Capitol album *Sinatra Sings . . . of Love and Things*. In 1991, it was added to the compact disc release of *Nice 'n' Easy*.

The song originated in Tin Pan Alley in early 1940. Glenn Miller and His Orchestra turned it into a hit. It has become an American standard.

Sinatra had recorded the song at Columbia on August 11, 1947, in a fine ballad arrangement by Axel Stordahl. The track is available on *Frank Sinatra—The Columbia Years 1943–1952* (CXK-48673-CK-52871) and on *Frank Sinatra: The Voice—The Columbia Years* (C4K-40343-CK-40631).

Sinatra rarely performed the song in concert.

$\mathcal{T}$he Johnny Mercer chestnut "Dream" was the first song scheduled for the March 2, 1960, recording session in Los Angeles. On the first take, Sinatra had trouble with a high note and wasted little time in telling Nelson Riddle, "That's a high mother. That's for Clark Dennis." On the second take, he stopped abruptly, and announced, "Next tune." Riddle replied, "How about 'She's Funny That Way'?" Sinatra finished "She's Funny That Way" in ten takes. At the end of the evening, Riddle composed a new chart for "Dream." It was recorded the following evening. The process involved in a Sinatra session was fluid for both the singer and arranger.

71

"I've Got a Crush on You"

Words by Ira Gershwin and music by George Gershwin
Recorded March 3, 1960, in Los Angeles
Arranged by Nelson Riddle
CD: *Nice 'n' Easy* (CDP 7-96827-2) and *Frank Sinatra—The Capitol Years* (C2-94777 CDP 7-94320-2)

A song Sinatra sank his teeth into at Columbia Records on November 5, 1947—and never let go. His original interpretation was terrific, but it pales in comparison to the recording at Capitol.

His voice in 1960 was simply richer and more commanding. Sinatra's reading is noteworthy for the clever way he segues from Ira Gershwin's amusing verse into a sensitive treatment of the chorus. The singer is backed by the pure romantic sound that had become Nelson Riddle's signature.

On the original Columbia recording, Sinatra was backed by a lush arrangement by Axel Stordahl and an outstanding trumpet solo by Bobby Hackett. The track is available on *Frank Sinatra—The Columbia Years 1943–1952* (CXK-48673-CK-52873) and on *The Voice—The Columbia Years* (C4K-40343-CK-40633).

The song was composed by the Gershwins for the 1928 Broadway musical *Treasure Girl*, performed by Mary Hay and Clifton Webb. It was also featured in the 1930 musical *Strike Up the Band*. The tune got off to a slow start, but gradually grew into a classic.

A concert recording by Sinatra, taped January 26 to February 1, 1966, is available on *Sinatra at the Sands* (Rep. CD 1019-2). A recording was made on July 6, 1993, at Capitol for *Duets* (CDP 0777-7-89611-2). Sinatra also recorded the song for the film *Meet Danny Wilson* on June 21 and July 11 of 1951 with the vocal quartet the Ebonaires. The track from June 21 was rejected.

Sinatra would perform the song in the forties, fifties, sixties, eighties, and nineties. A compelling version was done for a *GE Theater* television tribute to the Gershwins that aired on January 15, 1961, in which host Richard Rodgers introduced Sinatra as "the least sentimental and the most outstanding practitioner of the love song."

A glitch in the *Duets* recording of "I've Got a Crush on You" by Sinatra and Streisand was rescued by digital technology. Streisand had referred to Sinatra as "Francis" on the recording and wanted reciprocity, but Sinatra had already completed his segment. On August 24, 1993—backstage at the Sands in Atlantic City—Sinatra digitally recorded a new line for the song that included the name "Barbra." The line was subsequently edited into the recording.

72

"When the World Was Young"

Words by Johnny Mercer and music by M. Philippe-Gerard
Recorded September 11, 1961, in Los Angeles
Arranged by Axel Stordahl
CD: *Point of No Return* (CDP 7-48334-2) and *Frank Sinatra Sings the Select Johnny Mercer* (CDP 0777-7-80326-2)

A recording from *Point of No Return,* Sinatra's swan song album for Capitol Records. He had come full circle. His first session at Capitol was with arranger Axel Stordahl. His farewell LP would be with his old friend and mentor. The album is a collection of great standards. Romantic nostalgia is a common thread running through each song. Stordahl's sentimental arrangements bring an innocence to Sinatra's interpretations.

In this bittersweet song of remembrance, Sinatra delivers a graceful and wistful reading. His vocal is warm and intimate. His baritone is rich and embellishes the marvelous melodic line. This is Sinatra as master storyteller, weaving a tale of yesterdays when, indeed, the world was young.

Johnny Mercer created the song by anglicizing the French lyrics of Angela Vannier. The original French title was "Le Chevalier de Paris (Les Pommiers Doux)." Peggy Lee introduced Mercer's translation in 1950. A cabaret favorite, it was recorded by many pop artists, including Nat King Cole.

There are no known concert versions of the song by Sinatra.

(*Authors' Note*: Capitol plans to issue a complete boxed set of CDs in the near future.)

THE
REPRISE
YEARS

Authors' note: All of the following twenty-nine Reprise recordings have been released on a twenty-CD set, *Frank Sinatra: The Complete Studio Recordings*, Rep. CD 46013-2.

73

''In the Still of the Night''

Words and music by Cole Porter
Recorded December 19, 1960, in Los Angeles
Arranged by Johnny Mandel
CD: *Ring-a-Ding-Ding* (Rep. CD 9-27017-2)

A supercharged vocal by Sinatra in his prime. Here he takes a lovely ballad by Cole Porter and alters it dramatically. The driving swing arrangement by Johnny Mandel is played by a terrific group of jazz musicians. Sinatra gives an inspired performance. The last of five takes is done in all-out fashion.

Ring-a-Ding-Ding is Sinatra's first album for his own label, Reprise Records, where he would hang his hat for the next thirty years. The album is pure swing, and the songs are some of the finest ever composed. However, the project did not go smoothly. The original engineer was injured before the sessions were scheduled to begin and a hectic search was conducted for an eleventh-hour substitute. There were problems with the arrangements and some of the numbers were dropped at the last minute. In an interview in 1991, guitarist Al Viola reflected on the sessions: ''It's amazing how great an album it turned out to be, especially when you consider all the problems that we had."

"In the Still of the Night" was composed for the film musical *Rosalie* in 1937 and introduced by Nelson Eddy. It was a hit single for Tommy Dorsey and His Orchestra, with Jack Leonard on vocal. Later that year, it was a moderate hit for Leo Reisman and His Orchestra. Louis B. Mayer is said to have been moved to tears when he first heard the song.

A swinging concert recording is available on *Sinatra and Sextet: Live in Paris* (Rep. CD 9-45487-2), captured on June 5, 1962.

There is an unissued live recording of the song by Sinatra at the Sands Hotel in Las Vegas from November 5, 1961. Sinatra often performed the song in concert, right into the 1990s.

---

*T*he song "Zing Went the Strings of My Heart" had been recorded by Sinatra on December 21, 1960, for the album *Ring-a-Ding-Ding*. But Sinatra ordered the tape destroyed. From the beginning, he could not get a handle on the arrangement. After the third take, the tempo was slowed, and everyone seemed pleased with the final take, except Sinatra. Fortunately, before Sinatra's order was carried out, a copy was surreptitiously made. The tape was discovered in 1990 by Scott Sayers, a collector in Austin, Texas. It was subsequently mastered and added to the *Ring-a-Ding-Ding* compact disc (Rep. CD 9-27017-2). It is also available on *The Reprise Collection* (Rep. CD 9-26340-2).

---

*O*n December 22, 1960, Sinatra and Riddle secretly convened at a small studio in Los Angeles to record three songs: "The Last Dance," "The Second Time Around," and "Tina." The sub-rosa recording session at Sound Enterprise Studio was necessitated by a stipulation in Riddle's Capitol contract that prevented him from working with Sinatra at Reprise. The Reprise work sheets still claim that the session was held the previous evening.

74

"Polka Dots and Moonbeams"

Words by Johnny Burke and music by James Van Heusen
Recorded May 2, 1961, in Los Angeles
Arranged by Sy Oliver
CD: *I Remember Tommy* (Rep. CD 9-45267-2) and *Sinatra Sings the Songs of Van Heusen and Cahn* (Rep. CD 9-26723-2)

"Polka Dots and Moonbeams" was originally a pop hit for Tommy Dorsey and His Orchestra, with a young Frank Sinatra on vocal, recorded on March 4, 1940, to an arrangement by Axel Stordahl. It was the first Sinatra recording to hit the charts.

In the spring of 1961, Sinatra paid tribute to his great mentor by recording an album containing a collection of Dorsey's greatest hits with Sinatra, plus the band's theme song, "I'm Getting Sentimental Over You." For the project, Sinatra recruited a fellow Dorsey band alumnus, Sy Oliver, an outstanding arranger and musician who had written a number of uncredited swing charts for Sinatra during the singer's Columbia years. A thirty-seven-piece orchestra backed the former "boy singer" and the result is nothing short of sensational.

Of Sinatra's performance on this particular recording, jazz critic Gene Lees, writing in *HiFi/Stereo Review*, probably said it best: "If you listen to his 'Polka Dots and Moonbeams' . . . you will hear peerless phrasing for the meaning of the lyrics, you'll hear some remarkably controlled singing, with beautiful in-tune and well-sustained lines so long that you wonder if he's ever going to pause for breath." Although Sinatra's singing is impeccable throughout the album—an album of varied material—his performance on this ballad is the crowning moment.

Sinatra's original recording of the song in 1940 is available on *The Song Is You* (RCA 07863-66353-2). He performed the song many times with the Dorsey band in the early 1940s. There is an unreleased studio recording from March 20, 1961, at Reprise Records.

---

*S*inatra sings as if he is double-parked on his last two swing albums at Capitol Records. He was simply fulfilling his contract. His performances on *Sinatra's Swingin' Session* and *Come Swing with Me* are perfunctory for the most part. None of the twelve tracks on *Swingin' Session* run for more than three minutes— and half run for less than two. Nelson Riddle admitted in 1984 that Sinatra had instructed him to cut the running times in half on *Swingin' Session*. In 1991, Billy May was more diplomatic than Riddle—describing Sinatra's work on *Come Swing with Me* as very professional.

75

"You're Nobody 'til Somebody Loves You"

Words and music by Russ Morgan, Larry Stock, and James Cavanaugh
Recorded May 23, 1961, in Los Angeles
Arranged by Billy May
CD: *Swing Along with Me* (Rep. CD 1002-2) and *The Reprise Collection* (Rep. CD 9-26340-2)

A grand-slam performance by Sinatra with the help of an old friend. The singer is reunited with Billy May, whose arrangement gradually builds to a driving climax, allowing Sinatra to clear the bases.

The *Swing Along with Me* album is their fourth together. The later swing albums at Capitol are poor imitations of the work created here by Sinatra and May. Sinatra is never better than on such classics as "Falling in Love with Love,"

"Have You Met Miss Jones?" "Love Walked In," and nine more. The early years at Reprise are certainly on a par with Sinatra's best Capitol work.

The song was written in 1944 and made popular by Russ Morgan and His Orchestra in 1946. A marvelous recording by the Mills Brothers established the song as a standard. Through the years, it has been recorded by hundreds of recording artists.

A memorable version of the song was performed by Sinatra on his December 7, 1966, TV special *A Man and His Music II*. He introduces the song this way: "Right now, here's one of the greatest saloon songs since the Temperance League blew it, baby." The vocal is infectious and the performance is a joy to watch, available on a Warner Bros. video and a laser disc. A great concert recording is available on *Sinatra and Sextet: Live in Paris* (Rep. CD 9-45487-2). A recording of the song taped on November 5, 1961, from the Sands Hotel remains in the Reprise vault.

Sinatra performed the song in concert throughout the 1960s. His few renditions of the tune in the seventies and eighties lacked the liveliness of earlier performances.

---

*T*he Capitol album *Come Swing with Me!* and Reprise album *Swing Along with Me* were both released in mid-summer of 1961. They both climbed into the Top 10 on the *Billboard* album chart. This upset Capitol, which sued Reprise, claiming that the Reprise title was meant to confuse record buyers. The suit was upheld in court. As a result, Reprise was forced to retitle its album *Sinatra Swings*. The feud may be part of the reason why

Sinatra blatantly trashed his last Capitol recording, *I've Gotta Right to Sing the Blues*, on March 6, 1962. Three decades later, Reprise reclaimed its original title on the CD release of the album.

76

"Don't Take Your Love from Me"

Words and music by Henry Nemo
Recorded November 21, 1961, in Hollywood
Arranged by Don Costa
CD: *Sinatra and Strings* (Rep. CD 9-27020-2) and *The Reprise Collection* (Rep. CD 9-26340-2)

A vocal tour de force by Sinatra that would remain in the Reprise vault for almost thirty years because of a contractual agreement with Capitol.

Sinatra and Strings was the singer's first ballad album for his new record label. The huge string arrangements are done by the incredibly talented Don Costa. The sound of Sinatra had never been richer, nor had the singer been more romantically persuasive.

"Don't Take Your Love from Me" was recorded twice by Sinatra in 1961. The first recording, at Capitol on March 20, is a swing version with a terrific Heinie Beau arrangement. The recording is available on *Come Swing with Me* (CDP 7-94520-2). As part of Sinatra's legal settlement with Capitol Records, reached in January 1962, Sinatra was prohibited from releasing any song that he had recorded in the prior five years at Capitol. This prevented Reprise from issuing the recording on the *Sinatra and Strings* album. In the mid-1980s, the recording showed up on an import, then was added to the compact disc release of *Sinatra and Strings* in 1991.

A tune composed in 1941 and introduced by Mildred Bailey, the song was a chart hit for Glen Gray and the Casa Loma Orchestra in 1944. A lovely song with imploring lyrics, it has remained a favorite over the years.

Sinatra rehearsed the song in the late 1980s, but he would not perform it in concert.

77

''Come Rain or Come Shine''

Words by Johnny Mercer and music by Harold Arlen
Recorded November 22, 1961, in Hollywood
Arranged by Don Costa
CD: *Sinatra and Strings* (Rep. CD 9-27020-2) and *The Reprise Collection* (Rep. CD 9-26340-2)

One of Sinatra's all-time great recordings—a song restructured by the singer and his arranger. Rising to the challenge of an extraordinarily complex and driving arrangement by Don Costa, Sinatra gives a masterful interpretation of the song's bluesy rhythm and simple declarative sentiments. In his interpretation of the song, Sinatra had defined the proper way of singing it.

The song had been composed for the 1946 all-black Broadway musical *St. Louis Woman*, introduced on stage by Ruby Hill and Harold Nicholas. The show was a modest hit. The song did not fare much better for Margaret Whiting and the Paul Weston Orchestra, nor for Helen Forrest and Dick Haymes, who recorded the song as a duet.

Sinatra had performed the song, with a conventional reading, on his *Old Gold* radio show on June 5, 1946. The piece was arranged by Axel Stordahl and appears on *Frank Sinatra—The V-Discs* (C2K-66135-CK-66137). Sinatra performed the song on the *Star Spangled Review*, hosted by Bob Hope, on May 27, 1950. It marked Sinatra's television debut.

A recording was also made on July 1, 1993, to the Costa arrangement. Sinatra gives an admirable performance. The track is available from Capitol on *Duets* (CDP 0777-7-89611-2).

---

*A*fter recording "Come Rain or Come Shine," Sinatra sent a demo copy to its composer, Harold Arlen, with a note that instructed him to "Play it loud!"

78

"The Girl Next Door"

Words and music by Hugh Martin and Ralph Blane
Recorded January 16, 1962, in Los Angeles
Arranged by Gordon Jenkins
CD: *All Alone* (Rep. CD 9-27022-2)

At Reprise, Sinatra recorded many of the same standards
he had recorded at Capitol. He would rarely top the original. "The Girl Next Door" is an exception. The warmth of
his phrasing and precision of his vocal on this track is a
high point from the January 1962 sessions. The tonal quality is Sinatra at the top of his game. His magnificent reading
of the verse is alone worth the price of the CD.

All Alone, the first Reprise album with Gordon Jenkins,
is a collection of waltzlike tunes. Even by 1962 standards,
the album was considered old-fashioned. Full string arrangements by Jenkins backed Sinatra on five Irving Berlin
classics and seven other tracks that smacked of the 1920s.
The original title cut, "Come Waltz with Me," a Cahn and
Van Heusen composition, was not released on the original
album, but was later added to the compact disc reissue.

"The Boy Next Door" was the original title of this song
when it was written for the landmark MGM musical *Meet
Me in St. Louis* in 1944. The great Judy Garland sang the
song in the film. It was the flip side of her hit single, *Have*

Yourself a Merry Little Christmas, which also came from the film.

At Capitol Records, Sinatra recorded "The Girl Next Door" on November 6, 1953, to a superb coarrangement written by George Siravo and Nelson Riddle. The recording is available on *Songs for Young Lovers and Swing Easy* (CDP 7-48470-2).

Sinatra performed the song on the November 24, 1965, NBC-TV special *A Man and His Music,* available on video and laser disc from Warner Bros., but he apparently never performed it in concert.

---

*S*inatra was more inventive and experimental in his early years at Reprise Records. Each of his first seven albums at Reprise was with a different arranger. In order, they were Johnny Mandel, Billy May, Sy Oliver, Don Costa, Neal Hefti, Robert Farnon, and Gordon Jenkins.

79

``At Long Last Love''

Words and music by Cole Porter
Recorded April 11, 1962, in Hollywood
Arranged by Neal Hefti
CD: *Sinatra and Swingin' Brass* (Rep. CD: 9-27021-2)

One of two great recordings of the song by Sinatra. This time, Nelson Riddle takes a backseat to the arrangement of Neal Hefti, the talented musician and songwriter who emerged as Sinatra's secret weapon in the early 1960s.

Even today, more than three decades after he created it, Hefti's chart for the great Cole Porter tune is refreshingly buoyant. Sinatra and brass never sounded better together. Hefti's work on *Sinatra and Swingin' Brass* is no minor achievement. Bill Miller, Sinatra's longtime piano player, considers *Swingin' Brass* to be Sinatra's finest up-tempo album at Reprise.

Porter composed the song under incredible circumstances: On October 24, 1937, Porter was seriously injured while horseback riding. His legs were crushed when his mount fell on top of him, and he composed some of the lyrics for the song while waiting for help to arrive. The song was introduced by Clifton Webb in the 1938 Broadway musical, *You Never Know*. The following year, long before his TV show made him a household name, Ozzie Nelson and His Orchestra scored a major hit with it.

Sinatra's recording of the song with Riddle for Capitol on November 20, 1956, is the vocal equivalent of the 1962 track. It is available on *A Swingin' Affair!* (CDP 7-94518-2).

The singer's love for Cole Porter's music is exemplified by the countless number of times he performed Porter's material. Sinatra sang *At Long Last Love* in concert for the better part of four decades. A concert track is available on *Sinatra and Sextet: Live in Paris* (Rep. CD 9-45487-2), featuring a small-group sound.

Perhaps inspired by Ella Fitzgerald, with whom he performed a medley, Sinatra gave one of his best performances of the song during *A Man and His Music+Ella+Jobim* TV show, broadcast by NBC on November 13, 1967. It is available on video and laser disc from Warner Bros.

---

*T*he *Swingin' Brass* sessions were originally scheduled for three nights. At the first session on April 10, 1962, Sinatra was in such great vocal form that he canceled the third session. Instead, he recorded six tunes at each of the two sessions.

80

``Pennies from Heaven''

Words and music by Johnny Burke and Arthur Johnston
Recorded October 3, 1962, in Los Angeles
Arranged by Neal Hefti
CD: *Sinatra-Basie* (Rep. CD 1008-2) and *The Reprise Collection*
  (Rep. CD 9-26340-2)

Sinatra and Count Basie recorded ten swing numbers in two nights in early October 1962. What many critics had felt would be a bad musical marriage—the fear being that Sinatra's lighter sound and Basie's hard swing edge would be like oil and water—proved to be just the opposite.

Sinatra matched the syncopated rhythms of the Basie contingent note for note. Bill Miller did piano fills for Basie that only hard-core jazz buffs may be able to detect. Working with Sinatra took Sonny Payne's drum work to higher ground: "Sinatra is the only singer who makes me swing," Payne later explained. Many years in the planning stage, the album marked the beginning of a long and mutually beneficial association.

Sinatra's reading here is an improvement over the earlier recording at Capitol with Nelson Riddle. The singer had mastered the art of punching harder on the swing tunes. Hefti's arrangement may be his best chart on the album. Sinatra jumps all over it. The singer gives a commanding performance in a near-staccato interpretation of a first-rate tune.

The song was written for the 1936 Bing Crosby film *Pennies from Heaven*. Crosby's recording became the number-one song in the country, remaining there for ten weeks. It was also a hit for Hal Kemp and His Orchestra, Jimmy Dorsey and His Orchestra, Teddy Wilson and His Orchestra with Billie Holiday, and other great artists of the 1930s. The song by Johnny Burke and Arthur Johnston became a musical cornerstone of the Great Depression. It acknowledged the clouds and rainy days of the time, but expressed a sense of great optimism for the future. It is popular music as transcendent art.

Sinatra's Capitol recording was cut on January 10, 1956, for the seminal album *Songs for Swingin' Lovers* (CDP 7-46570-2). This track is highly recommended. Sinatra's vocals and Riddle's arrangement are both very solid.

Sinatra performed the song in concert for the next fifteen years. In the early 1980s, a revitalized Sinatra put the song back into his act, and it became a showstopper. There is a memorable TV performance with the Count Basie Orchestra on *The Man and His Music*, which aired November 22, 1981. The performance is available on video and laser disc from Warner Bros.

---

*I*n an interview in 1984, Nelson Riddle did not hesitate in naming *The Concert Sinatra* as the album at Reprise that he considered to be his best work with Sinatra. "Frank worked very hard on that album," said Riddle. "I think it shows in the final results."

81

''I Have Dreamed''

Words by Oscar Hammerstein II and music by Richard
  Rodgers
Recorded February 19, 1963, in Hollywood
Arranged by Nelson Riddle
CD: *The Concert Sinatra* (Rep. CD 1009-2) and *The Reprise
  Collection* (Rep. CD 9-26340-2)

Sinatra's best performance on his first album in three years
with Nelson Riddle, *The Concert Sinatra*, and one of his very
best vocal performances at Reprise. A beautiful sentiment
is expressed with great emotional power, as Sinatra displays a magnificent vocal and Riddle provides one of his
finest ballad arrangements.

Although Riddle had contributed some uncredited
charts during Sinatra's early years at Reprise, the great
team had offered relatively little to the music world during
the first few years of the sixties. *The Concert Sinatra* was an
auspicious renewal. The sessions for this ambitious project
were done at the Goldwyn Studios in Hollywood. The recordings were made on four sound stages with a seventy-
three-piece orchestra. The sound would be big and bright
and wonderful. The songs for the album were the cream
of Broadway musicals, including ''My Heart Stood Still,''
''Ol' Man River,'' ''You'll Never Walk Alone,'' and ''Solil-
oquy.'' The concept was simple: Sinatra would give a re-

cital in a concert setting and the audience would be record buyers. It worked.

A classic love song from Rodgers and Hammerstein, the tune was composed for the 1951 Broadway musical hit *The King and I*. It was introduced on stage by Doretta Morrow and Larry Douglas.

Sinatra sang the song in concert for many years. A powerful concert performance at the Royal Festival Hall in London on November 16, 1970, is available on video and laser disc from Warner Bros.

82

``Luck Be a Lady''

Words and music by Frank Loesser
Recorded July 25, 1963, in Los Angeles
Arranged by Billy May
CD: *Sinatra Reprise—The Very Good Years* (Rep. CD 9-26501-
2) and *The Reprise Collection* (Rep. CD 9-26340-2)

"Luck Be a Lady" ranks right up there with "Skin" and "Tramp" as one of Sinatra's all-time great swing numbers. Billy May never wrote a better arrangement. With its irrepressible beat and unremitting energy, the chart drives Sinatra's vocal with all the subtlety of a Mack truck. It allows Sinatra to accomplish what he set out to do—to prove that he could sing this song better than anyone else.

Written in 1950 for the Broadway musical *Guys and Dolls*, the song was introduced by Robert Alda. The score for *Guys and Dolls* is one of the finest ever composed for the stage. Marlon Brando sang the tune in the 1955 film version.

Sinatra felt that he should have been cast in the Sky Masterson role in the Goldwyn film. Brando got the nod instead. In his role as Nathan Detroit, Sinatra got to sing several great numbers, but he wasn't fully satisfied. For one thing, he didn't get to sing "Luck Be a Lady."

Sinatra got his chance in the summer of 1963, on a four-LP set comprising complete Broadway scores, which he had conceived and produced. He enlisted the top talents at Reprise for the project. They included Bing Crosby, Rosemary Clooney, Dean Martin, Sammy Davis, Jr., Jo Stafford, and Keely Smith. The inclusion of the score from *Guys and Dolls* was an obvious choice.

Sinatra recorded the song again on July 9, 1993 for *Duets II* (CDP 7243-8-28103-2) with the Billy May arrangement. A concert track from the Sands engagement, January 26 to February 1, 1966, is done with a Billy Byers arrangement. It remains unissued.

Sinatra's fondness for the song shows in his concert performances. It was always a highlight. Usually he would do a playful reading of the verse. At the end of the song, he would call out the brief coda, "eleven," that would be in perfect sync with the arrangement. A live track from *A Man and His Music II*, which aired on December 7, 1966, is available on a Warner Bros. video and a laser disc.

---

*O*n July 10, 1963, Sinatra recorded the song "Guys and Dolls" in a duet with Dean Martin. At best, it is passable. Fortunately, it has never been released. Bill

Loose, the arranger, subsequently rewrote the chart, and eight days later Sinatra and Martin recorded a far superior version.

83

"The Way You Look Tonight"

Words by Dorothy Fields and music by Jerome Kern
Recorded January 27, 1964, in Los Angeles
Arranged by Nelson Riddle
CD: *Frank Sinatra/Academy Award Winners* (Rep. CD 1011-2)
   and *The Reprise Collection* (Rep. CD 9 26340-2)

A truly exceptional recording by Sinatra. Done in a light, swinging mood, the talents of Sinatra and Riddle make the song sparkle. The result is a definitive track.

Days of Wine and Roses, Moon River and Other Academy Award Winners is not only a tediously long album title, it is also a disappointing effort. The work is inconsistent and there are lapses. An example is "Secret Love." During the session, Sinatra says of it: "I'm not too thrilled with this song." Meanwhile, he passed up an opportunity to record with Riddle a classic like "Lullaby of Broadway," opting instead to record other selections that are closer to mediocrity than to greatness. "The Way You Look Tonight" is the one great track from the undertaking.

The tune was conceived for the 1936 film musical *Swing Time*, starring Fred Astaire and Ginger Rogers. Astaire sings the song to Rogers in the film. It was Astaire's biggest hit song, the number-one hit in the United States for six weeks and a mainstay on the charts for seventeen weeks. The song also was a hit for Guy Lombardo and His Royal Canadians, and for Teddy Wilson and His Orchestra with Billie Holiday on vocal. An eloquent composition by Jerome Kern and Dorothy Fields, it received the 1936 Academy Award for best song.

Sinatra's first take on the song was as a ballad in a V-Disc recording from a *Songs by Sinatra* dress rehearsal on November 21, 1943, available on *Frank Sinatra—The V-Discs* (C2K-66135-CK-66136). Axel Stordahl's appealing string arrangement is marred by the unnecessary choral backing of the Bobby Tucker Singers.

In 1989, the song was introduced to a new generation when Sinatra and the song were featured in a TV commercial for Michelob beer. In a nightclub setting, Sinatra lip-synched to the 1964 recording. The commercial generated many letters from fans asking Sinatra to perform the song in concert—and people at his shows began shouting for it. Although the song was added to the rehearsal schedule, it was never performed by Sinatra in concert.

84

``The Best Is Yet to Come''

Words by Carolyn Leigh and music by Cy Coleman
Recorded June 9, 1964, in Los Angeles
Arranged by Quincy Jones
CD: *Sinatra/Basie—It Might as Well Be Swing* (Rep. CD 1012-2) and *The Reprise Collection* (Rep. CD 9-26340-2)

An impeccable vocal from Sinatra from the second Sinatra/Basie album. The singer's syncopation to the beat of the Basie band and his flawless enunciation provide a tutorial on the art of popular singing.

The follow-up Sinatra/Basie album was inevitable. The arranger is Quincy Jones, who had worked with the Basie band before. Sinatra was now working with a new producer, Sonny Burke, who had inspired in the singer a new level of confidence. Burke had already done some A & R work for Sinatra and had produced the album *America, I Hear You Singing*, featuring Sinatra, Bing Crosby, and Fred Waring and His Pennsylvanians.

There is an interesting contrast in this Sinatra/Basie reunion. Sinatra worked the first session with the Basie band and just a few additional jazz musicians. On the other two nights, he fortified the group with a sixteen-piece string section. The initial session is vastly superior on all fronts. The arrangements jump and the singing is outstanding. Sinatra and Basie simply did not need strings.

The song was written in 1959 by Coleman and Leigh. There have been many great recordings of the song by pop and jazz artists through the years, beginning with Tony Bennett.

The song became a Sinatra staple in the late 1970s and remained in his act for the next sixteen years. A wonderful version with Count Basie was performed on *The Man and His Music* TV special, which aired on November 22, 1981. The recording is available on video and laser disc from Warner Bros. Sinatra recorded the song again on October 12, 1993, for Capitol's *Duets II* (CDP 7243-8-28103-2).

85

``It Was a Very Good Year''

Words and music by Ervin Drake
Recorded April 22, 1965, in Hollywood
Arranged by Gordon Jenkins
CD: *September of My Years* (Rep. CD 1014-2) and *The Reprise Collection* (Rep. CD 9-26340-2)

Sinatra at fifty. "It Was a Very Good Year" is a powerful, life-affirming statement. The singer brings a wistful interpretation to a piece of work that is strongly autobiographical. Looking back on a lifetime of incredible highs and lows, Sinatra sings with greater insight and feeling than ever before. The composer, Ervin Drake, was moved by Sinatra's wonderful treatment of his song, set to the hauntingly beautiful and brilliantly understated score of Gordon Jenkins. Drake later called Jenkins and thanked him.

The critics shared Drake's sentiments. The song earned Sinatra a Grammy for Best Male Vocal Performance. It earned Jenkins a Grammy for Best Arranger. The album *September of My Years* won the Grammy for Album of the Year.

"It Was a Very Good Year" was written in 1961 and introduced by the Kingston Trio as a folk song. Sinatra heard the song on the car radio while driving into Los Angeles, fell in love with it, and had it added to the sessions for *September of My Years*.

A concert recording by Sinatra is available on *Sinatra at the Sands*, recorded January 26 to February 1, 1966 (Rep. CD 1019-2). Sinatra positioned the song as the main piece of a marvelous medley for the television special *A Man and His Music*, broadcast on November 24, 1965. Available on a video and laser disc from Warner Bros., the singer introduces the song with the observation, "A lyric can be a lament, it can be an exclamation of joy, or a lyric can tell the sum and substance of a man's life."

---

*T*he *September of My Years* album quickly climbed the charts when it was released in July 1965. But by late September, sales leveled off, and it appeared the work was destined to become only a moderate hit. TV to the rescue. On November 16, 1965, CBS aired a television special called *Sinatra: An American Original*, which featured a clip of the recording session for the song "It

Was a Very Good Year." Almost overnight, the album shot back up the charts, where it remained for sixty-nine weeks. The Sinatra TV special holds the distinction of being the only show in American television history to outrank the popular series *The Fugitive* in its regular time slot.

86

"Moonlight Serenade"

Words by Mitchell Parish and music by Glenn Miller
Recorded November 29, 1965, in Hollywood
Arranged by Nelson Riddle
CD: *Moonlight Sinatra* (Rep. CD 1018-2) and *The Reprise Collection* (Rep. CD 9-26340-2)

Sinatra's last great ballad album with Nelson Riddle was *Moonlight Sinatra*. Unfortunately it was dismissed by many critics when it was released in March 1966. They felt the moon concept was too gimmicky. Regardless of the concept, the work by Sinatra and Riddle is glorious. It may be the best singing Sinatra did in the mid-1960s. And Riddle's charts—on songs like "Moonlight Becomes You," "I Wished on the Moon," "Moon Love" and others—possess a dreamy quality that sets the stage for Sinatra's seductive interpretations.

On the ultimate "June and swoon" song, "Moonlight Serenade," Sinatra's vocal is strikingly exquisite. From the start, he was determined to get it right. Before take one, he is caught on tape saying, "Gee, this is a nice tune." After an aborted take, he proclaims, "If we don't get this one, I'm going to cry." He didn't get that one, but on take eleven it all fell into place.

There may be no song that better evokes the sound of the big-band era than "Moonlight Serenade." An earlier version of the tune was titled "Now I Lay Me Down to Sleep" with words by Edward Heyman. The retitled version was done in 1939. It became Glenn Miller's theme song.

Through the years, Sinatra performed a number of "moon songs" on radio, television and in concert—but "Moonlight Serenade" would not be one of them.

87

"Fly Me to the Moon"

Words and music by Bart Howard
Recorded January 26 to February 1, 1966, in Las Vegas
Arranged by Quincy Jones
CD: *Sinatra at the Sands* (Rep. CD 1019-2)

Sinatra live, at his swinging best. A Quincy Jones arrangement and the big driving sound of the Count Basie band propels Sinatra's vocal into musical outer space. As the Count plays the anticipatory vamp behind him, the Voice makes an irreverent aside to the audience, then shifts into musical overdrive.

Sinatra at the Sands may have been the most anticipated album of Sinatra's career. Never before had there been a concert or nightclub performance available on commercial record. When the album was released, in August 1966, it moved quickly into the *Billboard* Top 10. It remained a bestseller for forty-four weeks. The selections on the album are the best of Sinatra's repertoire, including "I've Got You Under My Skin," "Where or When," "Angel Eyes," "One for My Baby," "You Make Me Feel So Young," and "It Was a Very Good Year," plus a lovely "Shadow of Your Smile," for which no Sinatra studio recording exists. Nevertheless, the LP was an artistic disappointment. It was done at the end of a four-week engagement and the fatigue in Sinatra's voice is noticeable on many of the tracks. The work also suffers from its disjointedness—and from an interminable and unnecessary monologue. Still, it holds a special place in the hearts of many Sinatra fans.

The song was written in 1954, introduced by Felicia Sanders and first recorded by Kaye Ballard. For many years, the song was known as "In Other Words." Mabel Mercer made it a cabaret favorite and Joe Harnell and His Orchestra enjoyed a hit with the song in 1962.

"Fly Me to the Moon" was first recorded by Sinatra on June 9, 1964, in an outstanding version that may be the best arrangement Quincy Jones ever charted for Sinatra. It is available on *Sinatra/Basie—It Might as Well Be Swing* (Rep. CD 1012-2) and on *The Reprise Collection* (Rep. CD 9-26340-2). By January 1966, it had become a Sinatra staple.

Sinatra recorded the song again on October 12, 1993 for Capitol's *Duets II* (CDP 7243-8-28103-2). The arrangement borrows from the original Quincy Jones chart with additional work by Patrick Williams. It will be remembered for being the last recording by Antonio Carlos Jobim, Sinatra's duet partner on the track. An unreleased live track from Sinatra's retirement concert of June 13, 1971, remains in the Reprise vault.

Sinatra kept the song in his act for more than thirty years, sometimes using it to open concerts. A notable performance was done for the TV special *A Man and His Music II,* on December 7, 1966, available on video and laser disc from Warner Bros.

---

*S*inatra was "along for the ride" during the historic Apollo 11 mission that culminated in the first manned landing on the moon on July 20, 1969. While orbiting the lunar surface, the astronauts beamed back to Earth the Sinatra song "Fly Me to the Moon."

88

"Summer Wind"

Words by Johnny Mercer and music by Henry Mayer
Recorded May 16, 1966, in Hollywood
Arranged by Nelson Riddle
CD: *Strangers in the Night* (Rep. CD 1017-2) and *The Reprise Collection* (Rep. CD 9-26340-2)

Sinatra had wanted a hit single for a long time and, in April 1966, he got a monster: "Strangers in the Night." It became the biggest worldwide hit of his fifty-six-year career. In the wake of the British rock invasion, "Strangers in the Night" was the first single to knock the Beatles from the top of the American charts. The following month, Sinatra and Riddle rushed to the studio to record an album built around the hit single. The album shot to number one and remained on the charts for seventy-three weeks. Sinatra would win the Grammy for best male vocal performance and Ernie Freeman would win a Grammy for arrangement of the title track. In addition, Sinatra would pick up Album of the Year honors for the Reprise double album *A Man and His Music.*

The follow-up single to *Strangers in the Night* was a respectable hit but never came close to achieving the commercial success of its predecessor. Riddle's arrangement utilized a jazz organ, giving the song a modern sound. The midtempo chart found the perfect groove for the sound of Sinatra in 1966, and a wonderfully melodic line worked to enrich the knowing cynicism in Sinatra's vocal. Today, the giant hit from the mid-1960s is little more than a golden oldie, while the follow-up single is well positioned to become a timeless classic.

"Summer Wind" originated in West Germany, with lyrics composed by Hans Bradtke. In 1965, Johnny Mercer penned the English lyrics. The song was recorded by Wayne Newton and Perry Como.

Sinatra recorded the song again, on July 6, 1993, for the Capitol *Duets* project (CDP 0777-7-89611-2) with the original Riddle arrangement.

In 1966 and 1967, Sinatra regularly performed the song in concert, then dropped it from the act. The song resurfaced in 1984, back by popular demand after the song was played over the credits in the movie *The Pope of Greenwich*

Village. Sinatra promptly reinserted the song into his repertoire, where it remained well into the 1990s. It was a consistent crowd pleaser, rocking a concert hall with its electricity, the audience clapping in time to the driving tempo as Sinatra skillfully turned up the intensity with each line.

---

*S*inatra's multidimensional vocal capability is never more apparent than on the song "That's Life." A major hit for him in 1966 despite the overzealous choral backing, the recording is performed in a near growl by the singer. On December 7, 1966, Riddle modified Ernie Freeman's original chart to create a marvelous version that aired on the CBS-TV special *A Man and His Music II*. The track is available on video and laser disc from Warner Bros.

89

``I Concentrate on You''

Words and music by Cole Porter
Recorded January 30, 1967, in Hollywood
Arranged by Claus Ogerman
CD: *Francis Albert Sinatra and Antonio Carlos Jobim* (Rep. CD
1021-2) and *The Reprise Collection* (Rep. CD 9-26340-2)

The Sinatra/Jobim project, in the winter of 1967, may be Sinatra's single greatest work at Reprise Records. Certainly it ranks with his seven or eight greatest concept albums. The seductively pulsating sound of the bossa nova exported to the United States from Brazil by Jobim and others in the early sixties was a relatively short-lived craze. But the quality of the songs will assure a lasting legacy for Jobim and his musical genre.

Sinatra was late in coming to this music. The vocal demands required the utmost in breath control, phrasing, and intonation—no small task for a fifty-one-year-old singer. The German arranger Claus Ogerman constructed his twenty-piece orchestra around Jobim's guitar and Brazilian drummer Dom um Romao. A light yet unrelenting Latin beat created a romantic motif that inspired not only Sinatra but the musicians as well. Jobim's songs made up seven of the ten tracks on the album. It is a beautiful work with just a tinge of sadness. On this particular cut, Cole Porter's music blends magically with the sound of Jobim,

Ogerman's arrangement is wonderfully quiet, and Sinatra is superb. The result is a minor masterpiece.

The song was written in 1939 for the MGM film musical *Broadway Melody of 1940*. Although intended for Fred Astaire, the song was introduced by Douglas McPhail, with Astaire and Eleanor Powell dancing to the tune. In 1940, the song was a minor hit for both the Tommy Dorsey Orchestra and the Eddy Duchin Orchestra.

"I Concentrate on You" was a Sinatra standard for the better part of four decades. He first recorded it on January 9, 1947, for Columbia Records. Axel Stordahl mixed some brass instruments with his trademark string sound and Sinatra provided a strong interpretation. The recording is available on *Frank Sinatra—The Columbia Years 1943–1952* (CXK-48673-CK-52871) and on *Frank Sinatra—Hello Young Lovers* (CGK-40897). A swing version was done at Capitol on August 22, 1960, to an orchestral chart written by Nelson Riddle. This track is available on *Sinatra's Swingin' Session! and More* (CDP 7 46573-2) and on *Frank Sinatra Sings the Select Cole Porter* (CDP 7-96611-2).

A memorable performance was aired on the NBC television special *A Man and His Music + Ella + Jobim* on November 13, 1967. It is sung by Sinatra with Jobim as part of a medley from the Sinatra/Jobim album. The track is available on video and laser disc from Warner Bros.

---

*S*onny Burke, producer of some of Sinatra's finest Reprise albums, when asked a decade later his opinion of Sinatra's work with Jobim, replied: "Great! Frank sang the hell out of those tunes."

90

"Dindi"

Words and music by Ray Gilbert, Antonio Carlos Jobim, and
  Aloysio de Oliveira
Recorded January 30, 1967, in Hollywood
Arranged by Claus Ogerman
CD: *Francis Albert Sinatra and Antonio Carlos Jobim* (Rep. CD
  1021-2) and *The Reprise Collection* (Rep. CD 9-26340-2)

The Sinatra/Jobim album contains some of the loveliest
ballads ever composed, including "Quiet Nights," "Medi-
tation," "How Insensitive," "Change Partners," and "The
Girl from Ipanema." None is lovelier than "Dindi."

Jazz critic Gene Lees, lyricist for "Quiet Nights," wrote
about the Jobim recording sessions for *Stereo Review* in May
1967. His observations about "Dindi" are right on the
mark: "A Jobim song called 'Jingi' [phonetically correct]
sends chills up my arms and back. Sinatra's reading of it is
one of the most exquisite things ever to come out of American popular music. It is filled with longing. It aches. Some-
where within him, Frank Sinatra aches. Fine. That's the
way it's always been: The audience's pleasure derives from
the artist's pain."

Written in 1965, "Dindi" has been recorded by many
artists in the last thirty years, including a notable interpretation by Sarah Vaughan. Sinatra would not perform the
song outside the recording studio.

*S*inatra was still in "Jobim voice" when he recorded a duet with his daughter, Nancy, at the conclusion of his last session with Jobim on February 1, 1967. The song, "Somethin' Stupid," became Sinatra's biggest American hit of the sixties. When the tune was later dubbed "the incest song," Sinatra was not amused.

91

"Drinking Again"

Words by Johnny Mercer and music by Doris Tauber
Recorded February 1, 1967, in Hollywood
Arranged by Claus Ogerman
CD: *The World We Knew* (Rep. CD 1022-2) and *The Reprise Collection* (Rep. CD 9-26340-2)

Again, Sinatra uses the recording studio as theater. The singer acts out every excruciating moment of this dark piece, caressing every note in a manner not unlike self-confession. Sinatra walks a razor's edge between gloom and drunkenness as he brings to life Johnny Mercer's last great saloon song.

One can only wonder why Sinatra did not build a "saloon album" around this song. His singing in the winter of 1967 was impeccable, and he certainly was not lacking for similar tunes. A battle between the great artist and the successful pop singer may have been raging inside the singer.

If so, the pop singer won out. Sinatra would pass up many outstanding projects during this time, choosing instead to record tunes that catered to the commercial palate of the late sixties.

The tune was written in 1962 and recorded by Dinah Washington the following year. It has been covered by many recording artists.

Unfortunately, Sinatra's recording of "Drinking Again" is buried on an album of mediocre pop ditties, *The World We Knew*. In effect, it is a throwaway. Sinatra performed the song in concert a few times in the latter part of 1968.

---

*B*illy May and Bill Miller flew up to Seattle in September 1967 to meet with the Duke Ellington band. They gave the band the charts for the forthcoming Sinatra/Ellington album and left with assurances that the Ellington band would break the arrangements in on tour. They never did. This lack of preparation is apparent on a number of the charts on the album.

92

"Indian Summer"

Words by Al Dubin and music by Victor Herbert
Recorded December 11, 1967, in Hollywood
Arranged by Billy May
CD: *Frank Sinatra–Duke Ellington/Francis A. and Edward K.*
(Rep. CD 1024-2) and *The Reprise Collection* (Rep. CD 9-26340-2)

Songs that evoke strong visual imagery—like "Indian Summer"—brought out the best in Sinatra. Here he paints an ephemeral picture: "A ghost of a romance in June, fading away and ending too soon." The singer conveys the regrets of something fleeting, but tempers it with the wisdom that comes with age. The metaphorical implications of Indian summer are a source of great melancholy. This is personified by the mesmerizing alto sax solo by Johnny Hodges. Sinatra was so caught up with the magic of it that he almost forgot to come in again with his vocal. Listen carefully, and you will detect the slight delay.

One of Sinatra's all-time great vocals, "Indian Summer," arranged by Billy May, was Nelson Riddle's favorite Sinatra recording.

The song was written in 1939, from a Victor Herbert piano composition done in 1919. Sinatra sang the song with the Tommy Dorsey Orchestra in the early 1940s, but no known recording exists from a radio broadcast.

Sinatra never performed the Ellington chart in concert.

$\mathcal{S}$inatra produced a total of 1,414 studio recordings from 1939 to 1995. This includes V-Discs, film recordings, and studio work for record companies. It does not include promo work or concert recordings. More than one third of these total recordings were done at Reprise Records.

93

"Wave"

Words and music by Antonio Carlos Jobim
Recorded February 11, 1969, in Hollywood
Arranged by Eumir Deodato
CD: *Sinatra and Company* (Rep. CD 1033-2) and *The Reprise Collection* (Rep. CD 9-26340-2)

A tender and sensual reading by Sinatra to a light Latin beat from arranger Eumir Deodato. It is one of ten songs on the album *Sinatra/Jobim,* recorded in the wake of the critical and commercial success of their first endeavor.

The ten songs are all Jobim compositions, charted by Deodato. They include "Song of the Sabia," "One Note Samba," "This Happy Madness," and "Someone to Light Up My Life." The album was set for a January 1970 release. However, just prior to the actual release, Warner Bros. and Reprise Records decided to put *Sinatra/Jobim* (Rep. 1028) on the back burner. Instead, they chose to release *Watertown*, a conceptual album of ten songs written specifically for Sinatra. From an initial pressing of 450,000, Reprise sold 35,000 copies of the album. Meanwhile, *Sinatra/Jobim* was released piecemeal, with the exception of one track, "Desafinado" ("Off-Key"), which was released on *Frank Sinatra: The Complete Studio Recordings* (Rep. CD 46013-2).

"Wave" was composed by Jobim in 1960 and became a bossa nova favorite. It was the title track of a Jobim album released in the United States in 1968. There are many outstanding recordings of the song.

Sinatra rarely listens to his own work. He enjoys classical music. When he does listen to popular artists, he prefers Ella Fitzgerald, Tony Bennett, and Sarah Vaughan to his own recordings. An exception was "Wave." During his retirement in the early 1970s, Sinatra played the track over and over again at his compound in Palm Springs, California. A friend asked him why. He told her that he loved listening to the way he hit the bass notes.

The studio recording is Sinatra's only known performance of the song.

---

*I*n January 1970, the ill-fated *Sinatra/Jobim* album (Rep. 1028) was issued on eight-track tape just prior to the recall order. Subsequently, Reprise frantically hunted down copies and demanded that they be returned. Through the years, collectors have gone to incredible lengths to obtain this rare item.

94

``All My Tomorrows''

Words by Sammy Cahn and music by James Van Heusen
Recorded February 18, 1969, in Hollywood
Arranged by Don Costa
CD: *My Way* (Rep. CD 1029-2)

Sinatra teams with arranger Don Costa to perfect a song that Sinatra had initially recorded with Nelson Riddle over ten years earlier. Costa's beautifully understated string arrangement gives Sinatra the means to convey an intimacy and guarded sense of optimism that is inherent in the song. Together, Sinatra and Costa create a recording of quiet elegance.

``All My Tomorrows'' celebrates the indomitable spirit of man that Ernest Hemingway described when he wrote: ``A man can be destroyed but not defeated.'' This paradoxical view of existence is eloquently expressed in the recording. Sinatra and Riddle admirably captured it in the 1958 recording, but it pales in comparison to the treatment of the song by Sinatra and Costa in 1969.

The song had been commissioned by Sinatra in 1958 for his starring role in Frank Capra's comedy and penultimate film *A Hole in the Head*. Cahn and Van Heusen complied, and Sinatra recorded the song at Capitol on December 29, 1958, to an arrangement by Riddle. The recording, played over the opening credits of the film, was issued on the album *All the Way* (CDP 7-91150-2: currently out of print). The song is available on *Sinatra 80th—All The Best* two-CD set (CDD 7243-8-35952-2) from Capitol Records.

That Sinatra called upon Sammy Cahn and James Van Heusen in a pinch was not unusual. Over three decades, Cahn and Van Heusen wrote hit songs for Sinatra, theme tracks for his concept albums, music for his films and his TV appearances, plus a host of parodies and rewrites of songs written by other composers—all for Sinatra's consumption.

Sinatra taped a special promo recording of the song at United Artists in February 1959. An edited version was aired on radio to promote the film. Reportedly Sinatra performed the song a few times in concert in the late 1950s, but no tapes are known to exist.

---

*R*ecorded on December 30, 1968, "My Way" was to become one of Sinatra's most popular signature songs. The highest position it achieved on the *Billboard* Top 100 was number twenty-seven, clinging to the charts for only eight weeks. Opinion about the song is mixed: some view it as a personal anthem of great strength, others as an embarrassing self-congratulatory statement. Sinatra attempted to retire the song several times—but the fans simply wouldn't let him.

95

``Forget to Remember''

Words by Vincent Pike and music by Teddy Randazzo
Recorded August 18, 1969, in Hollywood
Arranged by Don Costa
CD: *The Reprise Collection* (Rep. CD 9-26340-2)

A decade after ``A Cottage for Sale,'' another dark torch song from Sinatra. A stunning vocal in light of Costa's big arrangement, Sinatra displays incredible control throughout a demanding piece, successfully walking a fine line between utter despair and false bravado. It is a delicate balancing act that Sinatra works to perfection. Because of his legendary recordings from the 1950s and early 1960s, Sinatra's great studio work in 1969 is often overlooked.

The song was written in 1969 and recorded by Sinatra as the B side to the forty-five RPM single, ``Goin' Out of My Head.'' The A side fell from the music charts after one week—it was overarranged and oversung. ``Forget to Remember'' was a song ill-suited for 1969. Songs of reflection and self-pity had become taboo in the free-spirited atmosphere of the late sixties. The ethos of the era had simply lost its ear for songs—even a definitive one—that portray the anguish of a severed relationship.

A terrific performance of the song by Sinatra was featured on the CBS-TV special *Sinatra 69*, broadcast on November 5, 1969. The track is available on video and laser disc from Warner Bros.

Sinatra's concert performances of the song were confined to the late sixties.

---

*W*atertown was the only major Sinatra album not to crack the *Billboard* Top 100. A great work that was badly packaged, poorly promoted, and finally left for dead, it deserved a far better fate. Together, the individual tracks on this concept album tell a modern love story with a theme of a broken marriage and shattered family. The more you play it, the better it gets.

96

``Just as Though You Were Here''

Words by Edgar De Lange and music by John Benson Brooks
Recorded September 24, 1974, in Hollywood
Arranged by Gordon Jenkins
CD: *The Reprise Collection* (Rep. CD 9-26340-2)

A very special recording from a fallow period for Sinatra. Here he reaches back to find the magic sorely missing from many of his recordings of the mid-1970s. To a wonderfully restrained chart by Gordon Jenkins, Sinatra brings a depth of feeling, a quiet heroism, and an almost mystical solace in his reflection on a ghost from the past.

The recording was made for a "saloon album" that was never completed. It would remain unreleased for sixteen years. When a collector informed Reprise Records of its existence, the song was issued on the four-CD *Reprise Collection* in 1990.

In the mid-1970s, Sinatra was struggling in the recording studio, although he continued to sell out concert halls around the world. He was trying to do contemporary material and, at the same time, not compromise the Sinatra sound. His best vocals (songs like "Send in the Clowns" and "There Used to Be a Ballpark") suffered from too much orchestration. By 1976, his voice simply wasn't the same. He was sixty-one.

"Just as Though You Were Here" was composed in 1942 and recorded by the Tommy Dorsey Orchestra with vocals by Frank Sinatra and the Pied Pipers. This song of loss and yearning was an immediate hit, striking a chord with the prevailing sense of profound upheaval that characterized the war years. The home front in World War II was struggling to come to terms with the dislocation of literally millions of Americans serving overseas. The track is available on *The Song Is You* (RCA 07863-66353-2). A radio air check is available on the same CD.

There are other live recordings of the song performed by Sinatra in the early forties with Dorsey, but he would never sing the 1974 version in concert.

97

``My Shining Hour''

Words by Johnny Mercer and music by Harold Arlen
Recorded September 17, 1979, in Los Angeles
Arranged by Billy May
CD: *Trilogy: Past, Present & Future* (Rep. CD 2300-2) and *The Reprise Collection* (Rep. CD 9-26340-2)

Trilogy: The Past is Sinatra's foremost album of the last quarter century. The songs are a tribute to the big-band sound, with outstanding charts by Billy May. But, above all, the album marked the return of Sinatra.

With the same kind of determination he had exhibited as an apprentice to Tommy Dorsey, Sinatra went back to school. He overhauled his singing style. With Robert Merrill, the opera singer, as his teacher, Sinatra learned to sing more from his ``bellows'' and to project his voice with much greater authority. The results were astonishing. He sounded twenty years younger.

Trilogy was the brainchild of Sonny Burke. In the late seventies, Sinatra had become estranged from the music scene. He rarely recorded and seldom released what he did record. He canceled a number of recording sessions—and walked out on one in early 1979. That spring, Burke presented the *Trilogy* idea to Sinatra, a concept that allowed the singer to return to the great standards that were best suited for his style. Fortunately, Sinatra listened.

"My Shining Hour" is Billy May's favorite track from the album. Sinatra's reading of the verse is delivered with great feeling and sensitivity. May uses a choral backing (à la the Pied Pipers) in a judicious manner. This allows Sinatra a forum to give a definitive interpretation. The song would be one of four cuts from the album to feature a choral backing.

There is an unreleased recording of the song from two months earlier, taped on July 16. In fact, Sinatra had recorded a total of nine songs at the July sessions. After listening to the results, he decided he could do much better on most of them. In September, he returned to the studio and redid seven of the nine tracks.

The song was written by Harold Arlen and Johnny Mercer for the 1943 Fred Astaire musical *The Sky's the Limit*. It was introduced in the film by Joan Leslie, with vocal dub by Sally Sweetland. That same year, it was a hit for Glen Gray and His Casa Loma Orchestra.

A Sinatra radio performance of the tune for his *Vimms Vitamins Show* of January 12, 1944, was recorded for V-Disc with an arrangement by Axel Stordahl. The track is available on *Frank Sinatra: The V-Discs* (C2K-66135-CK-66136). Sinatra also performed the song on *Your Hit Parade* in 1944. There are no known concert recordings.

What may be the greatest collaborative team in the history of American music ended on March 14, 1977—the last recording session of Frank Sinatra and Nelson Riddle. The singer and his arranger laid down three tracks: "Linda," "Sweet Lorraine," and a vocal overdub of "Barbara." Sinatra would later record "Something" on December 3, 1979 and "The Gal That Got Away" on April 8, 1981—but the arranger would not be present in the studio for the sessions. Together, Sinatra and Riddle created 318 recordings—223 at Capitol, 95 at Reprise.

98

"New York, New York"

Words by John Kander and music by Fred Ebb
Recorded September 19, 1979, in Los Angeles
Arranged by Don Costa
CD: *Triolgy: Past Present & Future* (Rep. CD 2300 2) and *The Reprise Collection* (Rep. CD 9-26340-2)

The ultimate anthem to the Big Apple, and a song that Sinatra doggedly worked on until he got it absolutely right. The process took eleven months.

He first performed the song in public on October 13, 1978, at the Waldorf-Astoria in New York for the Mercy Hospital Benefit. For the next several months, it would be the opening number in his act, then it became the show-stopper. The Sinatra camp was soon besieged with requests from fans for Sinatra to record the song.

Sinatra did so in New York on August 20, 1979. The chart was written by Don Costa, with Vinnie Falcone doing a great vamp on the piano. But Sinatra wasn't satisfied. He wanted to do it again—with more intensity. At this point, the song had been evolving for more than ten months. What started out as a tune with a moderate tempo had become, by September 1979, a declaration of defiance.

For Sinatra, the recording is a defining moment in a career of defining moments. Three months shy of his sixty-fifth birthday, Sinatra nails notes that are a stretch for many singers half his age. Costa's arrangement may be the finest of his celebrated career. Pete Jolly replaced Vinnie Falcone on piano to allow Falcone to conduct the session.

The song was written for the 1977 Martin Scorsese film *New York, New York,* starring Robert De Niro and Liza Minnelli. Minnelli introduced the song in the film. Although it appeared on a soundtrack album, and was later released as a single, the song never took off.

Sinatra recorded the song for *Duets* (CDP 0777-7-89611-2) on July 6, 1993.

Over the next fifteen years, Sinatra closed hundreds of performances with the song. A marvelous rendition was performed by Sinatra for the NBC-TV special *The Man and His Music,* broadcast on November 22, 1981. The track is available on video and laser disc from Warner Bros.

"*N*ew York, New York" became the unofficial anthem of New York City in 1980. As spring turned into summer, the song was heard on the streets, in taxis, in subways, in restaurants, in sports arenas. It became the mantra for the New York Yankees. When Carnegie Hall announced that Sinatra would play a two-week engagement in mid-June, the line to buy tickets at the box office was three deep and very long. He was again "king of the hill, top of the heap."

99

"The Gal That Got Away/ It Never Entered My Mind"

Words by Ira Gershwin and music by Harold Arlen/Words
   by Lorenz Hart and music by Richard Rodgers
Recorded April 8, 1981, in Hollywood
Arranged by Nelson Riddle and Don Costa
CD: *She Shot Me Down* (Rep. CD 2305-2) and *The Reprise
   Collection* (Rep. CD 9-26340-2)

Since 1973, Sinatra had been struggling to piece together an entire album of saloon songs. It was finally decided that all previous efforts be scrapped. A fresh start began with the session of April 8, 1981. Sinatra's impeccable recording of this medley underscores the fact that he had already perfected it. This song within a song had first been performed by Sinatra at Caesar's Palace in Las Vegas on August 25, 1977.

The arrangement is a perfect marriage between a modified chart Nelson Riddle had written in 1954 for "The Gal That Got Away" and a piano chart composed by Don Costa for "It Never Entered My Mind."

She Shot Me Down was Sinatra's last stellar album. It is a work of great craftsmanship. The tunes are contemporary, yet they address the age-old themes of love and lost love. The weary vocal of a man in his mid-sixties conveys a deeper and more mature portrait of acceptance and resignation.

"The Man That Got Away" (original title) was written for the 1954 Warner Bros. musical *A Star Is Born*. It was introduced in the film by Judy Garland and became a Garland classic. "It Never Entered My Mind" was written in 1940 for the Broadway musical *Higher and Higher*. Shirley Ross introduced the song in the play.

Sinatra recorded "The Gal That Got Away" at Capitol Records on May 13, 1954, with a Riddle arrangement. A slightly bigger hit than Garland's, the recording is available on *This Is Sinatra 1953–1957* (DL-1275), a double-CD set issued by EMI in England.

Sinatra's first recording of "It Never Entered My Mind" was done for Columbia Records on November 5, 1947. It is an excellent ballad version with a superb Stordahl arrangement, available on *Frank Sinatra—The Columbia Years 1943–1952* (CXK-48673-CK-52873) and on *The Voice—The Columbia Years* (C4K-40343-CK-40634). A magnificent recording for Capitol was done on March 4, 1955, featuring a far more profound reading by Sinatra. This time, the bitter irony of Hart's lyrics did not escape the singer. Riddle's carefully crafted arrangement provides a melancholy tone that fits the concept of the album—*In the Wee Small Hours* (CDP 7-96826-2). The track is also available on *Frank Sinatra Sings the Select Rodgers and Hart* (CDP 0777-7-80323-2).

Sinatra performed the medley throughout the eighties and into the nineties.

*W*ith the success of the *Trilogy* album and the hit single "New York, New York," Sinatra became the most enduring entertainer in the history of pop music. He had placed songs on the charts for five decades. Thirteen years later, he would have the number two album on the pop charts (*Duets*, selling more than six million copies), increasing his record to six decades. On his seventy-ninth birthday, *Duets II* was on the *Billboard* Top 10, the thirty-eighth Sinatra album to reach that plateau.

100

"Hey Look, No Crying"

Words by Susan Birkenhead and music by Jule Styne
Recorded September 10, 1981, in New York City
Arranged by Gordon Jenkins
CD: *She Shot Me Down* (Rep. CD 2305-2)

On the evening of September 10, 1981, Frank Sinatra sang at Carnegie Hall. The show was a rousing success, and the singer received several standing ovations. Immediately after the show, Sinatra climbed into a limo and was taken to the Columbia B recording studio in midtown Manhattan. There he completed his last album at Reprise, laying down the final two tracks: "Monday Morning Quarterback" and "Hey Look, No Crying."

There is no self-pity or self-serving sentimentality in Sinatra's interpretation of "Hey Look, No Crying." He sings it with great conviction. If he is haunted by a ghost from the past, he does not let us know it. Perhaps the memories are enough to sustain him. But when he sings the line, "me, I'm flying," it breaks your heart. "When I heard it, I cried. I really cried," said the lyricist, Susan Birkenhead. "It was a staggering experience. It was so completely overwhelming."

Sinatra chose to omit the following verse from the song. Birkenhead shared it with *Sinatra 101*:

> *I've just been told that the curtain's coming down*
> *The leading lady's even leaving town*
> *The leading man is shaken as you see*
> *Hell yes! But it's a question of degree*

In the early eighties, Sinatra regularly performed the song in concert, always with great feeling and with great respect for the lyric. An unedited alternate version of the song is available on *Frank Sinatra: The Complete Studio Recordings* (Rep. CD 46013-2).

---

*L*yricist Susan Birkenhead tells the story about how she came to write "Hey Look, No Crying" for Frank Sinatra:

In 1981, I was writing with Jule Styne. He and I were doing a musical together. It was fairly early in my career, and in my collaborative efforts with Jule. He called me on a Friday in early September. He said, "Frank is doing an album." I said, "Frank who?" He said, "*Frank!* He is doing an album of saloon songs, and he wants us to write a song about a guy whose woman left him. I'm sending the cassette over and we have to get it to him by Tuesday." I'm basically a theater writer. I had never written a pop song. I sat there for a while numb. Then my husband said, "Why don't you just pretend you're writing for a character and the character is Sinatra. You have the circumstances, so go." That's exactly what I did. He recorded it that week.

101

"It's Sunday"

Words by Susan Birkenhead and music by Jule Styne
Recorded February 28, 1983, in Los Angeles
Arranged by Tony Mottola
CD: *The Reprise Collection* (Rep. CD 9-26340-2)

We end on a quiet note. "It's Sunday" was written for Sinatra in the late fall of 1982. Don Costa gave the composition an elaborate arrangement and Sinatra recorded it on January 19, 1983 (unissued). During the playback, Sinatra just shook his head. He felt it needed a smaller sound. Tony Mottola ran it down with just his guitar. At the end of a session six days later, Sinatra did one take of the song as a reference tape, with Mottola on guitar. He liked what he heard.

In late February, Sinatra went back into the studio and recorded the song again. It is the only Sinatra recording ever done with just guitar.

The intimate sound provided by Mottola inspired Sinatra to render a lovely interpretation filled with warmth and great intimacy. Sinatra's syncopation is exceptional, particularly on the final chorus. For anyone who has ever spent a lazy Sunday with someone special—filled with newspapers and conversation and gentle affection—the moment has forever been captured by Sinatra.

The songwriting team of Styne and Birkenhead struck a chord in Sinatra that elevated his work. Jule Styne, a friend of Sinatra's for more than fifty years, had provided the singer with tunes since the early 1940s, including "Time After Time" and "Five Minutes More." Susan Birkenhead was the kind of lyricist Sinatra had desperately lacked for so many years. They shared an aesthetic sensibility and an affinity that manifested itself in pure recording artistry. Sinatra recognized the affinity and soared with it.

Sinatra performed the song in concert with Tony Mottola in 1983.

---

*A*nd finally, the collectors' choice. Charles Pignone, president of The Sinatra Society of America, P.O. Box 269, Newtonville, NY 12128, conducted a private poll for *Sinatra 101*. Here is the Society's top fifteen favorite recordings by Sinatra.

1. "I've Got You Under My Skin" (1956)
2. "New York, New York" (1979)
3. "My Way" (1968)

  4. "Summer Wind" (1966)
  5. "The Lady Is a Tramp" (1956)
  6. "All the Way" (1957)
  7. "It Was a Very Good Year" (1965)
  8. "That's Life" (1966)
  9. "One for My Baby" (1993)
10. "Young at Heart" (1953)
11. "My Kind of Town" (1964)
12. "Guess I'll Hang My Tears Out to Dry" (1958)
13. "Fly Me to the Moon" (1964)
14. "Strangers in the Night" (1966)
15. "Come Fly with Me" (1957)

ABOUT THE AUTHORS

Ed O'Brien is one of the world's foremost authorities on Frank Sinatra. He is the author of four books on Sinatra. His work has been hailed as "definitive" by both *The Los Angeles Times* and *The Chicago Tribune*. He has written liner notes for several Sinatra albums. Recently, O'Brien completed work on a new Sinatra CD project for Warner Bros.

Robert Wilson entered publishing following a professional baseball career. His publishing credits include work as a political reporter, music critic, freelance writer and book editor. His freelance articles have appeared in newspapers and magazines in the United States and abroad.